GCSE
Success

Deborah Dobson,
Phil Duxbury,
Mike Fawcett and
Aftab Ilahi

Exam Practice Workbook

Number

Algebra

Ratio, Proportion and Rates of Change

Geometry and Measures

Probability

Statistics

Practice Exam

1 **(a)** Work out −4 + −3 [1 mark]

....

(b) Work out (−3 × −2) + (−5 × −3) [1 mark]

....

(c) Work out (−8 − −5) × (7 − 12) ÷ (−2 − 3) [1 mark]

....

2 Are the following **true** or **false**?

(a) −3 + −2 < −2 − +3 [1 mark]

....

(b) −5 − −7 = 11 + −9 [1 mark]

....

(c) −4 × −7 × −10 = 10 × −4 × 7 [1 mark]

....

(d) 26 ÷ 15 > −28 ÷ −15 [1 mark]

....

3 The temperature in New York is 8°C. It is 11°C colder in London.

(a) What is the temperature in London? [1 mark]

....

Moscow is three times colder than London.

(b) Work out the temperature in Moscow. [1 mark]

....

4 Given that 129 × 42 = 5418, calculate the following.

(a) 1.29 × 4.2 [1 mark]

....

(b) 12.9 × 420 [1 mark]

....

(c) 5418 ÷ 0.42 [1 mark]

....

(d) 54.18 ÷ 0.129 [1 mark]

....

5 Bethany has £40. Tomorrow she will be paid £150 but will pay £225 for a holiday.

(a) How much debt will Bethany be in? [1 mark]

....

Bethany's father gives her $\frac{2}{5}$ of the amount she is in debt.

(b) How much debt is Bethany in now? [2 marks]

....

Score **/16**

For more help on this topic, see Letts GCSE Maths Foundation Revision Guide pages 4–5.

1 Write down all the factors of 48 which are:

(a) odd numbers [1 mark]

....

(b) square numbers [1 mark]

....

(c) multiples of 6 [1 mark]

....

2 James is thinking of a number between 1 and 50. It is 4 more than a prime number and 4 less than a square number. It is also a multiple of 3.

What could James's number be? [2 marks]

.... or ....

3 **(a)** Find the lowest common multiple (LCM) of 5 and 11. [1 mark]

....

(b) Find the highest common factor (HCF) of 14 and 35. [1 mark]

....

4 **(a)** Write 72 as a product of its prime factors. Give your answer in index form. [3 marks]

....

(b) Write 90 as a product of its prime factors. Give your answer in index form. [3 marks]

....

(c) Find the highest common factor (HCF) of 72 and 90. [2 marks]

....

(d) Find the lowest common multiple (LCM) of 72 and 90. [2 marks]

....

5 Bus A leaves the bus station every 12 minutes.
Bus B leaves the bus station every 28 minutes.
Bus A and Bus B both leave the bus station at 8.00am.

When will they next both leave the bus station at the same time? [3 marks]

....

Score   /20

For more help on this topic, see Letts GCSE Maths Foundation Revision Guide pages 6–7.

Module 2

1 **(a)** Work out $5 + 2^2 \times 3$ 🖩 [1 mark]

....

(b) Work out $\dfrac{1}{5} + \dfrac{2}{5}$ 🖩 [1 mark]

....

(c) Write down the reciprocal of 4. 🖩 [1 mark]

....

2 Work out $\dfrac{(12 - 5 \times 2)^2}{5 - 3}$ .... [2 marks]

3 Calculate the following. Give your answers in their simplest form. 🖩

(a) $\dfrac{4}{5} \times \dfrac{3}{8}$ .... [2 marks]

(b) $\dfrac{5}{6} \div \dfrac{3}{10}$ .... [2 marks]

(c) $\dfrac{3}{4} - \dfrac{3}{5}$ .... [2 marks]

(d) $\dfrac{3}{5} + \dfrac{1}{3}$ .... [2 marks]

4 Wes is drawing storyboards for a new film. One day he completes $\dfrac{2}{5}$ of the drawings.

On the next day he completes $\dfrac{3}{7}$ of the drawings.

What fraction of the drawings has he got left to complete? 🖩 [3 marks]

....

5 A wall measures $1\dfrac{1}{4}$ m by $2\dfrac{2}{3}$ m.

Find the area of the wall, giving your answer as a mixed number. 🖩 [3 marks]

 .... m²

6 Tank A and Tank B are identical water tanks.

Tank A is $\dfrac{3}{5}$ full. Tank B is $\dfrac{2}{9}$ full.

Tank B is emptied into Tank A.

What fraction of Tank A is now empty? 🖩 [3 marks]

....

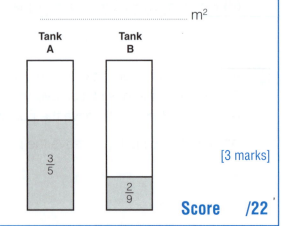

Score /22

For more help on this topic, see Letts GCSE Maths Foundation Revision Guide pages 8–9.

Operations

Module 3

1 Write the following in index form.

(a) $3 \times 3 \times 3 \times 3 \times 3 \times 3$ .... [1 mark]

(b) $12 \times 12 \times 12 \times 12$ .... [1 mark]

2 Write the following in order of value, smallest first.

2^5 $\qquad$ $\sqrt[3]{64}$ $\qquad$ 3^3 $\qquad$ 5^2 $\qquad$ $\sqrt[4]{625}$ $\qquad$ [1 mark]

....

3 Find the value of x in each of the following.

(a) $2^x = 128$ .... [1 mark]

(b) $\sqrt[3]{x} = 5$ .... [1 mark]

(c) $x^4 = 81$ .... [1 mark]

4 **(a)** Write $4^6 \div 4^4$ as a single power of 4.  [1 mark]

....

(b) Write $5^3 \times 5^{-5}$ as a single power of 5. 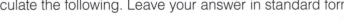 [1 mark]

....

(c) Write 3×10^{-4} as an ordinary number. 🖩 [1 mark]

....

5 **(a)** Write the following numbers in standard form. 🖩

(i) 321 000 .... [1 mark]

(ii) 0.000 605 .... [1 mark]

(b) Calculate the following. Leave your answer in standard form. 🖩

(i) $(5 \times 10^3) \times (6 \times 10^{-8})$

.... [2 marks]

(ii) $(4.1 \times 10^4) + (3.4 \times 10^3)$

.... [2 marks]

6 Work out the value of the following. 🖩

(a) 12^0 .... [1 mark]

(b) 4^{-2} .... [1 mark]

Score **/17**

For more help on this topic, see Letts GCSE Maths Foundation Revision Guide pages 10–11.

1 Write the following fractions as decimals. 🖩

   (a) $\frac{7}{10}$ .... [1 mark]

   (b) $\frac{15}{20}$ .... [1 mark]

   (c) $\frac{9}{25}$ .... [1 mark]

2 Write the following in order of value, smallest first.

   $\frac{12}{25}$ $\frac{3}{8}$ 0.475 $\frac{17}{51}$ [1 mark]

....

3 Write 56% as a fraction in its simplest form. 🖩   [1 mark]

....

4 Which of the fractions $\frac{5}{8}$ and $\frac{7}{11}$ is closest to $\frac{2}{3}$? Show your working. 🖩   [3 marks]

....

....

5 Calculate the following. 🖩

   (a) 3.7×4.9 [2 marks]

....

   (b) $56 \div 1.4$ [2 marks]

....

6 Carl orders 34 Creamy Crisp Doughnuts for a church event.

   Each doughnut costs £1.29

   Find the total cost of the doughnuts. Show your working. 🖩   [3 marks]

....

....

7 Find the decimal which is equivalent to $\frac{2}{9}$. 🖩   [1 mark]

....

Score   **/16**

For more help on this topic, see Letts GCSE Maths Foundation Revision Guide pages 12–13.

1 Round the following numbers to the degree of accuracy shown.

(a) 3549 to the nearest hundred .... [1 mark]

(b) 28.54 to the nearest whole number .... [1 mark]

(c) 699 to the nearest ten .... [1 mark]

2 Calculate the value of these numbers to the degree of accuracy shown.

(a) $\sqrt{90}$ (2 decimal places) .... [1 mark]

(b) 2.56^2 (3 decimal places) .... [1 mark]

(c) $\sqrt[3]{175.6}$ (2 decimal places) .... [1 mark]

3 **(a)** Round 404 928 to 2 significant figures. [1 mark]

....

(b) Round 0.04965 to 3 significant figures. [1 mark]

....

(c) Round π to 4 significant figures. [1 mark]

....

4 Estimate $\dfrac{23 \times 2.8}{0.5}$ 📱 [2 marks]

....

5 Violet runs a coffee lounge. She wants to make 34 cups of coffee from a 500g bag of coffee.

How much coffee should she use for each cup? Give your answer to 3 significant figures.

.... g [2 marks]

6 Rachel works in a school office. She sends, on average, 72 letters home each week. Each letter costs 59p to send. There are 39 weeks in the school year.

Estimate the cost of sending the letters home for the whole year. 📱 [3 marks]

£ ....

7 Ethan is 1.7m tall to 1 decimal place.

Write down the limits of accuracy for his height. [2 marks]

....

Score   /18

For more help on this topic, see Letts GCSE Maths Foundation Revision Guide pages 14–15.

Approximations

Module 6

1 Calculate the following. Write down all the figures on your calculator display.

(a) 4.5^4 .... [1 mark]

(b) $\sqrt[4]{2401}$ .... [1 mark]

(c) $\sqrt[7]{78125}$ .... [1 mark]

2 Calculate the following. Write down all the figures on your calculator display.

(a) $\dfrac{4+3.9^2}{5.2\times6.3}$ [2 marks]

(b) $\sqrt{4+3.1\times8}$ [2 marks]

3 (a) Work out $(3.5\times10^4)\times(4.9\times10^3)$ giving your answer in standard form. [1 mark]

(b) Work out $(4.56\times10^{-2})\div(3.8\times10^{-7})$ giving your answer in standard form. [1 mark]

4 Calculate the following using the fraction button on your calculator.

Give your answer as a mixed number.

(a) $14\frac{2}{3}-11\frac{5}{7}$ .... [1 mark]

(b) $4\frac{3}{10}\times7\frac{2}{9}$ .... [1 mark]

5 The Sun is 400 times further away from the Earth than the Moon.

The Sun is 1.496×10^8km away from the Earth.

(a) How far away is the Moon from the Earth? Write your answer in standard form. [3 marks]

.... km

The Moon has a diameter of 3.48×10^3km.

The Sun has a diameter of 1.392×10^6km.

(b) How many times bigger is the Sun's diameter compared with the Moon's diameter? Write your answer in standard form. [3 marks]

Score /17

For more help on this topic, see Letts GCSE Maths Foundation Revision Guide pages 16–17.

1 Simplify the following expressions. 📝

(a) $8a + 2 - 3a$ .... [1 mark]

(b) $6h + 3k + 9h - k$ .... [1 mark]

(c) $5a + 2b + 3c - 4a - 3a - 3c$ .... [1 mark]

(d) $3x^2 - 2x + 5x^2 + x + 1$ .... [1 mark]

2 Simplify the following expressions. 📝

(a) $3p^2 \times 2p^5$ .... [1 mark]

(b) $\left(3p^4\right)^3$ .... [1 mark]

(c) $18f^7 g^2 \div 3f^2 g$ .... [1 mark]

(d) $\left(2p^2\right)^{-3}$ .... [1 mark]

3 Simplify the following expressions where possible. 📝

(a) $60k^2 \div 5$ .... [1 mark]

(b) $\sqrt[4]{a^{12}}$ .... [1 mark]

(c) $\sqrt[3]{p^6} \times \sqrt[6]{p^3}$ .... [1 mark]

(d) $p^2 \times p^3 \times \sqrt{p^3}$ .... [1 mark]

4 Evaluate: 📝

(a) 4^{-1} .... [1 mark]

(b) $\left(\dfrac{2}{5}\right)^{-2}$ .... [1 mark]

(c) $32^{\frac{2}{5}}$ .... [1 mark]

(d) 16^0 .... [1 mark]

5 Which of the following are **equations** and which are **identities**? 📝

(a) $3x - 4 = (3x + 1) - (x - 5)$ .... [1 mark]

(b) $\dfrac{p+q}{pq} = \dfrac{1}{p} + \dfrac{1}{q}$ .... [1 mark]

(c) $x^2 + x^2 = 2x^2$ .... [1 mark]

(d) $x^2 + x^2 = x^4$ .... [1 mark]

(e) $\sqrt{a + b} = \sqrt{a} + \sqrt{b}$ .... [1 mark]

Score /21

For more help on this topic, see Letts GCSE Maths Foundation Revision Guide pages 20–21.

1 Simplify: 🔢

(a) $6(a - 2)$ [2 marks]

....

(b) $3m(m + 2)$ [2 marks]

....

(c) $4n(2n - p)$ [2 marks]

....

(d) $5(d + 1) + 3(d - 1)$ [2 marks]

....

(e) $8(x + 2) - 2(2x - 3)$ [2 marks]

....

2 Multiply out the brackets: 🔢

(a) $(a + 3)(a + 2)$ [2 marks]

....

(b) $(f + 6)(f - 5)$ [2 marks]

....

(c) $(x - 5)(x - 7)$ [2 marks]

....

(d) $(a + 4)^2$ [2 marks]

....

(e) $(a - 9)^2$ [2 marks]

....

3 Factorise: 🔢

(a) $3a - 3b$ [2 marks]

....

(b) $6p + 8$ [2 marks]

....

(c) $x^2 - 7x$ [2 marks]

(d) $2pq - 6q$ [2 marks]

(e) $5p^2 - 10p$ [2 marks]

4 Write $3(2x-1)+4(x+8)+5$ in the form $a(bx+c)$ where a, b and c are integers. [3 marks]

5 Factorise:

(a) $p^2 + 4p + 3$ [2 marks]

(b) $x^2 - 10x + 21$ [2 marks]

(c) $a^2 + 12a + 11$ [2 marks]

(d) $x^2 - x - 12$ [2 marks]

6 Factorise:

(a) $t^2 - 9$ [2 marks]

(b) $16 - f^2$ [2 marks]

(c) $1 - 25n^2$ [2 marks]

(d) $t^2 - 25$ [2 marks]

(e) $p^8 - 4$ [2 marks]

Score /51

For more help on this topic, see Letts GCSE Maths Foundation Revision Guide pages 22–23.

1 If $x = 4$, $y = -2$ and $z = 3$, find the values of:

(a) $(x - y)^2$ [1 mark]

(b) $\dfrac{x^2}{y}$ [1 mark]

(c) $2z - y$ [1 mark]

(d) $xy + z$ [1 mark]

(e) $\sqrt{10x + 2y}$ [1 mark]

2 Rearrange $v = u + at$ to make a the subject. [2 marks]

3 Rearrange $y = \dfrac{2 + x}{5}$ to make x the subject. [2 marks]

4 Rearrange $y = \dfrac{2 + 3x}{x - 8}$ to make x the subject. [3 marks]

5 A briefcase weighs p grams when empty. When it is full of q grams of paper, it weighs r grams. Write down an equation for q in terms of p and r. [2 marks]

6 The formula to convert degrees Fahrenheit to degrees Celsius is $T_C = \dfrac{5(T_F - 32)}{9}$

(a) Use this formula to convert 88 degrees Fahrenheit (T_F) to degrees Celsius. [1 mark]

(b) Rearrange this formula to make T_F the subject. [2 marks]

(c) Now convert 60 degrees Celsius to degrees Fahrenheit. [1 mark]

Score **/18**

For more help on this topic, see Letts GCSE Maths Foundation Revision Guide pages 24–25.

1 Solve the equation $4x - 7 = 29$ [2 marks]

....

2 Solve the equation $5(x-2)-3(x-4)=4$  [2 marks]

....

3 Solve the equation $\dfrac{x+4}{5} = \dfrac{x-2}{3}$ [3 marks]

....

4 Solve the equation $x^2 + 13x + 36 = 0$ [3 marks]

....

5 Solve, by factorisation, the equation $x^2 - 3x - 28 = 0$ [3 marks]

....

6 $4x - 3y = 14$ and $x + y = 7$, find the values of x and y. [4 marks]

$x =$ .... $\qquad$ $y =$ ....

7 $4x + 2y = 10$ and $3x + 4y = 10$, find the values of x and y. [4 marks]

$x =$ .... $\qquad$ $y =$ ....

8 The diagram shows the graph of $y = x^2 - 7x + 4$

(a) By using the graph, solve (approximately) the equation $x^2 - 7x + 4 = 0$ [2 marks]

....

....

(b) By using the graph, solve (approximately) the equation $x^2 - 7x - 4 = 0$ [2 marks]

....

....

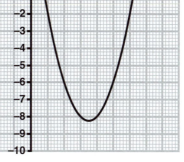

Score /25

For more help on this topic, see Letts GCSE Maths Foundation Revision Guide pages 26–27.

Module 11

1 Solve the inequality $7x - 2 > 33$ 🗊 [2 marks]

....

2 Solve the inequality $5 - 2x \geqslant x + 8$ [2 marks]

....

3 Solve the inequality $58 > 20 - 2x$ [3 marks]

....

4 State the inequalities as shown on the number lines below. 🗊

(a)  .... [1 mark]

(b) 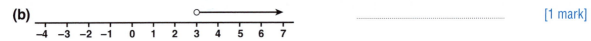 .... [1 mark]

(c) .... [1 mark]

5 List all integers x for which $-2 < x < 5$ 🗊 [2 marks]

....

6 List all integers x for which $-8 < x \leqslant -4$ 🗊 [2 marks]

....

7 List all integers x for which $3 \leqslant 2x \leqslant 13$ 🗊 [2 marks]

....

8 Solve the inequality $5 - 2x < 8x$, showing your solution on a number line. 🗊 [3 marks]

....

9 Find the integer value(s) of x for which $2x - 3 > 5$ and $12 - x > 6$ 🗊 [5 marks]

....

10 List all integers x for which $-2 < 10 - x < 7$ 🗊 [2 marks]

....

Score /26

For more help on this topic, see Letts GCSE Maths Foundation Revision Guide pages 28–29.

1 Here are the first four terms of an arithmetic sequence:

8   12   16   20

Write down the next two terms in the sequence.   [2 marks]

....

2 Here are the first four terms of an arithmetic sequence:

41   32   23   14

Write down the next two terms in the sequence.   [2 marks]

....

3 A term-to-term sequence is given by $U_{n+1} = 5U_n - 2$ where $U_1 = 1$

Write down the first five terms in this sequence.   [2 marks]

....

4 An arithmetic sequence has the formula $U_n = 9n - 1$.

Write down the first four terms in this sequence.   [2 marks]

....

5 11, 15, 19, 23, … are the first four terms in an arithmetic sequence.

(a) Find an expression for U_n, the position-to-term formula.   [2 marks]

....

(b) Is 303 a number in this sequence? Explain your answer.   [2 marks]

....

6 Here are the first four terms of an arithmetic sequence:

15   17   19   21

(a) The sequence may be expressed by using a term-to-term formula
$U_{n+1} = U_n + d$ with $U_1 = a$. Write down the values of a and d.   [2 marks]

$a =$ .... $d =$ ....

(b) Find an expression for U_n, the position-to-term formula.   [2 marks]

....

7 The position-to-term formula of a geometric sequence is given by $U_n = \left(\frac{1}{3}\right)^n$.
Write down the first four terms in this sequence.   [4 marks]

....

Score   **/20**

For more help on this topic, see Letts GCSE Maths Foundation Revision Guide pages 30–31.

Sequences

Module 13

1 Find the gradients of the following lines labelled A, B, C and D. 🖩 [4 marks]

A: $y = 6x - 7$ B: $y = 8 - 3x$

C: $2x + 3y + 4 = 0$ D: $y - x = 0$

Line A: Gradient is ....   Line C: Gradient is ....

Line B: Gradient is ....   Line D: Gradient is ....

2 From the following lines, write down the two that are parallel. 🖩 [2 marks]

A: $3y = x - 6$ B: $4x + 2y = 8$

C: $x = 3y - 12$ D: $2y - x + 2 = 0$

Lines .... and .... are parallel.

3 Write down the equation of the y-axis. [1 mark]

....

4 A line has gradient -6 and passes through the point $(0, 9)$.

Find the equation of the line. [2 marks]

....

5 Work out the equation of the line parallel to $y = 5x - 2$ that passes through the point $(-3, 1)$. [3 marks]

....

6 A parallelogram has one vertex in each of the four quadrants. Three of the vertices have coordinates $(1, 3)$, $(2, -1)$ and $(-3, 1)$.

By drawing a diagram, find the coordinates of the fourth vertex. [3 marks]

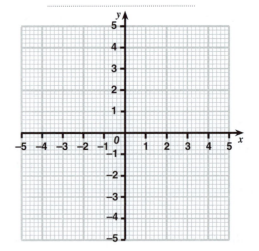

....

7 Find the equation of the line joining points $(-4, -10)$ and $(6, -5)$. [4 marks]

....

Score /19

For more help on this topic, see Letts GCSE Maths Foundation Revision Guide pages 32–33.

1 This is the graph of the quadratic curve $y = x^2 + 2x - 15$

Using the graph:

(a) Write down the roots of the
equation $x^2 + 2x - 15 = 0$ [2 marks]

$x =$ .... and

$x =$ ....

(b) Write down the coordinates of
the intercept with the y-axis.   [1 mark]

....

(c) Write down the coordinates of
the turning point on the graph.   [2 marks]

....

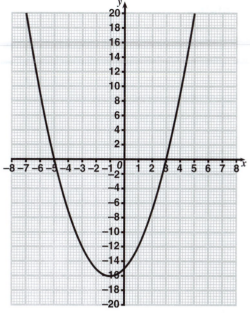

2 Find (using algebra) the roots of the equation $x^2 - 7x - 44 = 0$ [3 marks]

....

3 This is the graph of $y = 5 + 2x - x^2$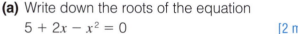

Using the graph:

(a) Write down the roots of the equation
$5 + 2x - x^2 = 0$ [2 marks]

$x =$ .... and $x =$ ....

(b) Write down the coordinates of the
intercept with the y-axis.   [1 mark]

....

(c) Write down the equation of the line of
symmetry of the graph.   [2 marks]

....

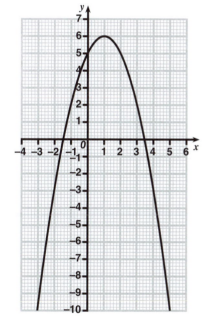

4 Consider the curve $y = x^2 - 8x + 3$. Without drawing the graph:

(a) Write down the equation of the line of symmetry of the curve.   [2 marks]

....

(b) Work out the coordinates of the minimum point on the curve.   [2 marks]

....

Score   **/17**

For more help on this topic, see Letts GCSE Maths Foundation Revision Guide pages 34–35.

1 For the function $f(x) = 12x + 5$, write down the outputs for each of the following inputs:

Input x   **Output $f(x)$**

  0   →   ....

  1   →   ....

  2   →   .... [3 marks]

2 Find the function given by the following mapping:

Input x   **Output $f(x)$**

  2   →   3

  3   →   6

  4   →   9   [2 marks]

....

3 For the function $f(x) = \dfrac{x+3}{2}$, write down the inputs for each of the following outputs:

Input x   **Output $f(x)$**

....   →   4

....   →   4.5

....   →   5   [3 marks]

4 **(a)** On the grid, sketch graphs of:

   (i) $y = x^3$ [2 marks]

   (ii) $y = \dfrac{1}{x}$ [2 marks]

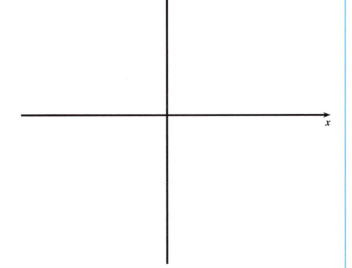

(b) Write down the number of solutions there are to the equation $x^3 = \dfrac{1}{x}$
(you do not have to find the solutions).   [1 mark]

....

5 Four different graphs are illustrated below. Match the correct line with its graph.

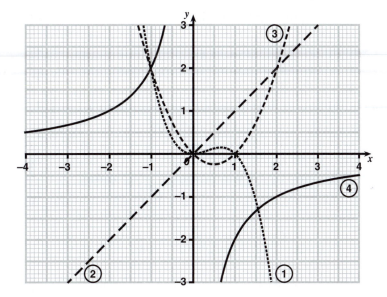

Choose from: $y = -\dfrac{2}{x}$, $y = x$, $y = x^2 - x^3$, $y = x^2 - x$ [4 marks]

Line 1 ....

Line 2 ....

Line 3 ....

Line 4 ....

6 Sketch the graphs of $y = \dfrac{2}{x}$ and $y = \dfrac{-4}{x}$ on the same axes. 🄕 [4 marks]

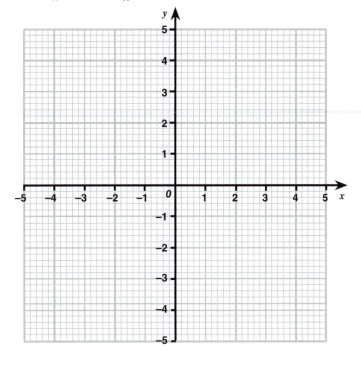

Score /21

For more help on this topic, see Letts GCSE Maths Foundation Revision Guide pages 36–37.

1 The following shows a distance–time graph for Max walking to college and back.

(a) If Max set off at 9.30am, what time did he reach college? [1 mark]

....

(b) For how long did Max stay at college? [1 mark]

....

(c) What was Max's speed on his way home? [2 marks]

....

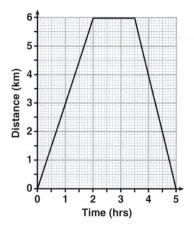

2 The following shows a speed–time graph for a train.

(a) Calculate the initial acceleration of the train. [2 marks]

....

(b) For how long was the train travelling with constant speed? [1 mark]

....

(c) How far did the train travel in the first 15 seconds? [2 marks]

....

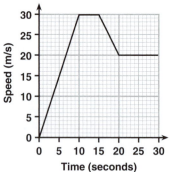

3 The following graph is used by a taxi firm to calculate the cost of a single journey.

(a) How much is the standing charge? [1 mark]

....

(b) How much does a journey of six miles cost? [1 mark]

....

(c) Work out the cost per mile that the taxi firm charges, not including the standing charge. [2 marks]

....

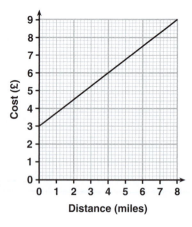

Score **/13**

For more help on this topic, see Letts GCSE Maths Foundation Revision Guide pages 38–39.

1 Calculate the area of a rectangle with width 850mm and length 1.25m. [2 marks]

....

2 Convert 3.4km^2 to metres^2. 🖩 [2 marks]

....

3 If 1cm^3 of water has a mass of 1g, what is the mass of 1m^3 of water in kilograms? 🖩 [2 marks]

....

4 5 miles = 8km

Which is faster, 68mph or 110km/h? [2 marks]

....

5 Convert 24m/s to kilometres per hour. [3 marks]

....

6 Shahida works 30 hours each week and earns £18.40/h.

Bob works 35 hours each week and earns £626.00.

Leila works 32 hours each week and earns £30 000 per annum.

(a) Who has the best hourly rate? [3 marks]

....

(b) Who earns the most per year? [2 marks]

....

7 Here are two pieces of gold:

Block A has a volume of 24cm^3 and a mass of 463g.

The volume of block B is 30cm^3 and it contains exactly the same quality of gold.

A   B

(a) Calculate the density of the gold. [2 marks]

....

(b) Calculate the mass of block B. [2 marks]

....

(c) If the price of gold is £23.50/g, calculate the total value of both pieces. [2 marks]

....

Score   /22

For more help on this topic, see Letts GCSE Maths Foundation Revision Guide pages 42–43.

Converting Measurements

Module 18

1 A model plane is made using a scale of 1 : 20

(a) If the wingspan of the model is 3m, what is the wingspan of the actual plane? [1 mark]

....

(b) If the plane is 57m long, how long is the model? [2 marks]

....

2 Here is a map with a scale of 1 : 5 000 000

(a) What is the distance on the map between Bristol and Leeds? [1 mark]

....

(b) What is the actual distance? [2 marks]

....

(c) Measure the bearing of Exeter from Leeds. .... [2 marks]

(d) What is the bearing of Leeds from Exeter? .... [2 marks]

3 A cruise ship sets off from harbour A for 100km on a bearing of 075° to point B. It then changes to a bearing of 220° and sails at 15km/h for 6 hours to point C. Finally it heads straight back to the harbour (A).

(a) Draw an accurate diagram to show the journey using a scale of 1cm : 20km   [2 marks]

(b) Measure the bearing and distance of the last leg of the journey from C to A.   [2 marks]

Bearing: ....   Distance: .... km

4 A map is drawn to a scale of 1 : 25000

Villages S and R are 18cm apart on the map.

(a) Work out the actual distance between S and R in kilometres.   [2 marks]

....

R is due West of S. T is another village. The bearing of T from R is 040° and the bearing of T from S is 320°.

(b) Draw a diagram to show the positions of S, R and T.   [2 marks]

Score   /18

For more help on this topic, see Letts GCSE Maths Foundation Revision Guide pages 44–45.

Scales, Diagrams and Maps

Module 19

1 Circle the numbers which are **not** equivalent to 3.75 📱 [2 marks]

$\dfrac{30}{8}$ 37.5%   375% $\dfrac{14}{5}$ $3\dfrac{5}{8}$ $\dfrac{750}{200}$

2 Write the following numbers in ascending order. 📱 [2 marks]

0.21   20% $\dfrac{3}{10}$ 0.211 $\dfrac{2}{9}$

3 Is 2.125 or $2\dfrac{4}{5}$ closer to $2\dfrac{1}{2}$? Explain your reasoning. 📱 [2 marks]

4 On a new estate of 32 houses, $\dfrac{3}{8}$ have two bedrooms. $\dfrac{5}{6}$ of the two-bedroom houses have a garage.

What percentage of the whole estate is represented by two-bedroom houses with a garage? [2 marks]

5 Claire makes soft toys to sell at a Christmas market.

(a) Each dog toy costs £3.45 to make and Claire sells them for £5.99.

What is her percentage profit? [2 marks]

(b) A tiger toy costs 15% more to make than a dog toy and she makes 80 tiger toys. Claire sells 55 of them for £6.99 and the rest at the reduced price of £4.

What percentage profit does she make on tiger toys? [4 marks]

6 At Mathstown School 55% of the students are girls. 40% of the girls and 65% of the boys have school lunch.

(a) What percentage of students at the school have school lunch? [3 marks]

(b) What fraction of the boys do not have school lunch? [2 marks]

Score   /19

For more help on this topic, see Letts GCSE Maths Foundation Revision Guide pages 46–47.

1 Simplify these ratios and circle the odd one out. You must show all your working. 🔲 [2 marks]

£4 : £6   10 : 15   20cm : 3m   750g : 1.125kg   40 seconds : 1 minute

....

....

....

2 Jane is making 'mist blue' paint for her room. She mixes navy blue, grey and white paint in the ratio 1 : 2 : 7

(a) How much of each colour does Jane need to make 2 litres of 'mist blue' paint? [3 marks]

Navy blue: .... ml   Grey: .... ml   White: .... ml

(b) Jane finds she has $\frac{3}{4}$ litres of navy blue, 1200ml of grey and 6 litres of white paint.

What is the maximum amount of 'mist blue' she can make? [2 marks]

.... litres

3 The ratio of A : B is 5 : 8

Complete this statement. A is ⬜/⬜ of B. 🔲 [1 mark]

4 This is a recipe for shortbread:

Makes 15 biscuits			
110g butter	50g sugar	175g flour	50g chocolate chips

(a) Amil has 70g of sugar. How many biscuits can he make? [2 marks]

....

(b) How much flour is needed to make 12 biscuits? [2 marks]

.... g

5 Lucy makes green paint by mixing yellow and blue paint in the ratio 5 : 2
Blue paint costs £30 for 5 litres and yellow paint costs £28 for 7 litres.

Lucy sells her green paint for £4.50 per litre. Will she make a profit? Show your working to justify your decision. 🔲 [3 marks]

....

....

....

Score   /15

For more help on this topic, see Letts GCSE Maths Foundation Revision Guide pages 48–49.

1 If Shabir has 250ml of soup for her lunch, how many kilocalories of energy will she get? .... [2 marks]

SOUP
100ml = 59kcal

2 Leon changes £500 to euros at the rate shown and goes to France on holiday.

£1 = 1.29 euros	*£1 = 187.99 Japanese yen*
£1 = 1.56 US dollars	*£1 = 97.04 Indian rupees*

(a) How many euros does he take on holiday? .... [1 mark]

Leon spends €570.

(b) He changes his remaining euros on the ferry where the exchange rate is £1 : €1.33

How much in pounds sterling does he take home? .... [2 marks]

3 Fred's dairy herd of 80 cattle produces 1360 litres of milk per day.

(a) If Fred buys another 25 cattle and is paid 30p/litre, what will his annual milk income be? .... [4 marks]

(b) If 6 tonnes of hay will last 80 cattle for 10 days, how long will the same amount of hay last the increased herd? [2 marks]

....

4 Similar triangles are the same shape. Triangles *PQR* and *STU* are similar.

Find the missing lengths *PR* and *TU*. [4 marks]

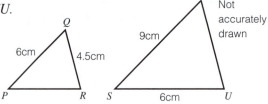

Not accurately drawn

PR = ...

TU = ...

5 Two similar cylinders P and Q have surface areas of 120cm² and 270cm².

(a) Calculate the scale factor of their areas. [1 mark]

....

(b) What is the scale factor of the heights of the two cylinders? [2 marks]

....

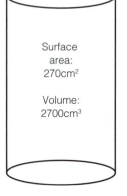

Q

Surface area: 270cm²

Volume: 2700cm³

P

Surface area: 120cm²

(c) If the volume of Q is 2700cm³, what is the volume of P? [3 marks]

.... cm³

Score /21

For more help on this topic, see Letts GCSE Maths Foundation Revision Guide pages 50–51.

1 (a) Peter invests £10 000 in a savings account which pays 2% compound interest per annum.

How much will his investment be worth after four years? [2 marks]

....

(b) Paul invests £10 000 in company shares.
In the first year the shares increase in value by 15%.
In the second year they increase by 6%.
In the third year they lose 18% of their value.
In the fourth year the shares increase by 1%.

What is his investment worth after four years? .... [3 marks]

2 Lazya invests £6500 at 3% compound interest for three years. She works out the first year's interest to be £195. She tells her family she will earn £585 over three years.

Is she right? Show working to justify your decision. [3 marks]

....

....

3 This graph shows a tank being filled with water and then emptied.

(a) How deep is the water when the tank is full?

.... [1 mark]

(b) Between what times is the tank filling fastest?

.... [1 mark]

(c) Work out the rate of decrease of water level as the tank empties. .... [1 mark]

4 This graph shows the distance travelled by a cyclist for the first 10 seconds of a race.

(a) What distance does the cyclist travel in the first 8 seconds? [2 marks]

....

(b) Work out the cyclist's average speed for the first 10 seconds. [2 marks]

....

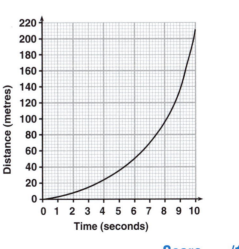

Score /15

For more help on this topic, see Letts GCSE Maths Foundation Revision Guide pages 52–53.

Rates of Change

Module 23

1 Using only a ruler and a pair of compasses, construct a triangle with sides 8cm, 7cm and 9cm.

[2 marks]

2 Using only a ruler and a pair of compasses, construct a rectangle with one side 8cm and an area of 28cm².

[2 marks]

3 Using only a ruler and a pair of compasses, draw a line PQ such that angle PQR is 90°.

[2 marks]

Q _____ R

4 This is a plan of a field using a scale of 1cm : 10m

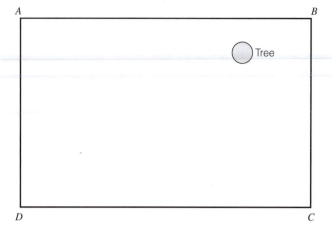

The farmer wants to install a water trough. It must be:

- at least 15m from the tree
- more than 20m from the fence *DC*
- nearer to *AB* than to *AD*.

Shade the area where the farmer can put the trough. [3 marks]

5 Using only a ruler and a pair of compasses, construct an angle of 30°. [3 marks]

Score /12

For more help on this topic, see Letts GCSE Maths Foundation Revision Guide pages 56–57.

1 Will a regular pentagon tessellate? Use a diagram in your explanation. [2 marks]

....

....

....

....

2 The internal angles of a regular polygon are 135°.

How many sides has the polygon? [2 marks]

....

3 *ABIJKL* and *BCDEFGHI* are regular polygons. Calculate angle *JIH*. [3 marks]

....

4 Calculate angle *FED*. State all your reasons. [3 marks]

....

....

....

....

5 Lines *BC* and *DE* are parallel. Calculate angle *CPR*, giving all your reasons. [2 marks]

....

....

Score /12

For more help on this topic, see Letts GCSE Maths Foundation Revision Guide pages 58–59.

1 Draw lines to match each triangle with its correct description. [3 marks]

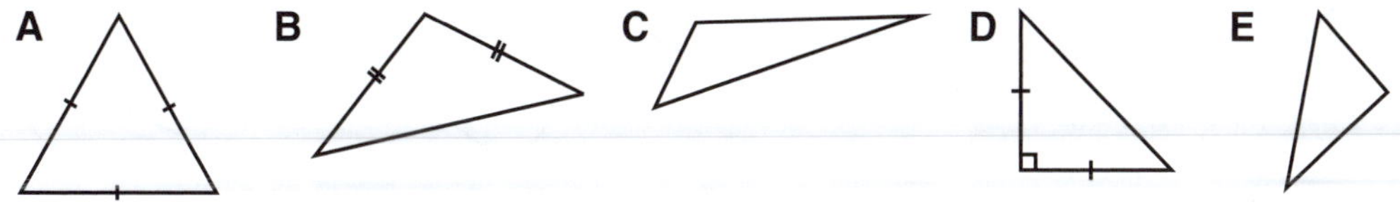

| A | B | C | D | E |

| Scalene | Right-angled isosceles | Equilateral | Obtuse scalene | Obtuse isosceles |

2 Use this diagram to prove the angle sum of a triangle is 180°. [3 marks]

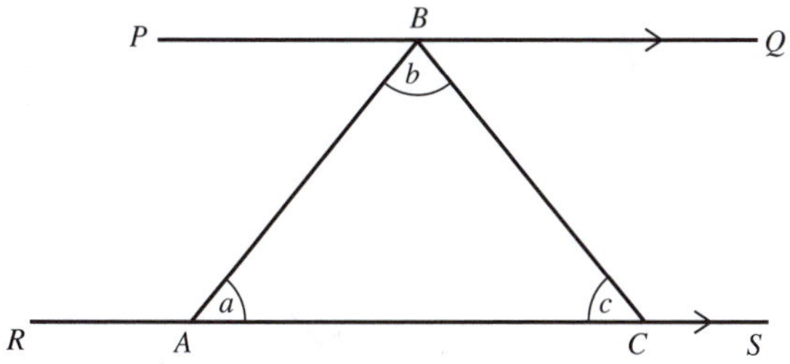

....

....

....

....

3 Use this diagram to find the angle sum of an octagon. [3 marks]

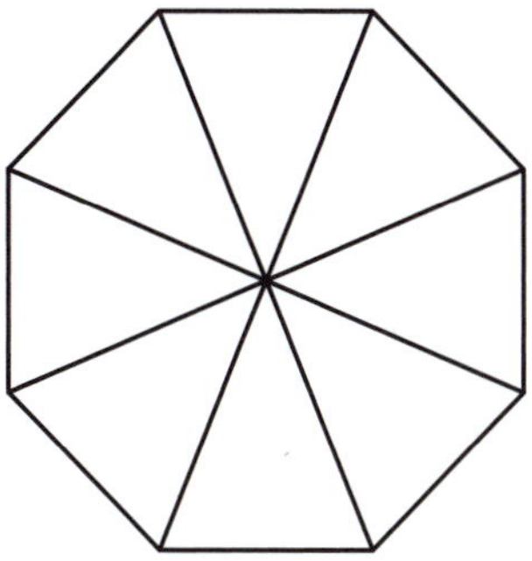

....

4 Complete this sentence with the name of the correct quadrilateral.

A .... has two pairs of equal sides but only one pair of equal angles. [1 mark]

5 Find angle x, giving all your reasons. [3 marks]

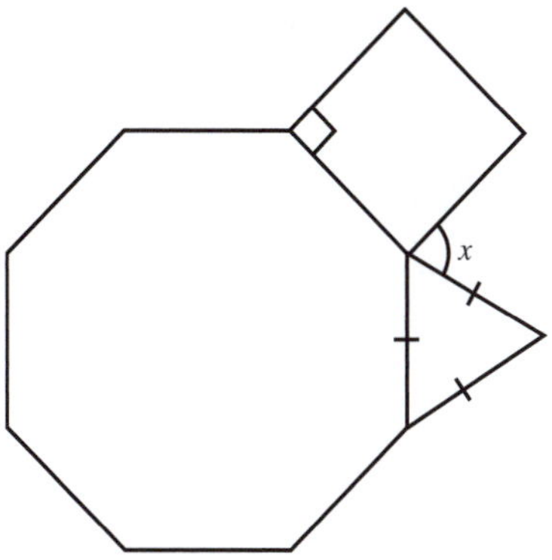

....

....

....

....

Score /13

For more help on this topic, see Letts GCSE Maths Foundation Revision Guide pages 60–61.

Properties of 2D Shapes

Module 26

1 Circle the two similar triangles. [1 mark]

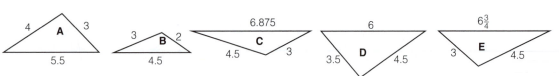

2 Circle the two congruent triangles. [1 mark]

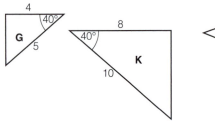
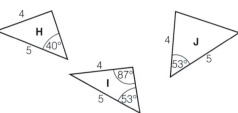

3 Triangle *FGH* and triangle *PQR* are similar.

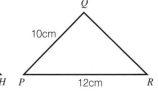

Calculate:

(a) *QR* [2 marks]

....

(b) *FG* [2 marks]

....

4 State whether these triangles are congruent and give your reasons. [2 marks]

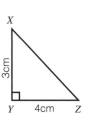
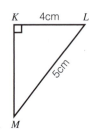

....

....

....

5 The dimensions of a £10 note are 142mm × 75mm and those of a £50 note are 156mm × 85mm.

Are the two notes mathematically similar? Explain your reasoning. [3 marks]

....

....

....

Score **/11**

For more help on this topic, see Letts GCSE Maths Foundation Revision Guide pages 62–63.

Congruence and Similarity

Module 27

1 (a) Describe the transformation
that moves A on to B. [2 marks]

....

....

(b) Describe the transformation that
moves B on to C. [2 marks]

....

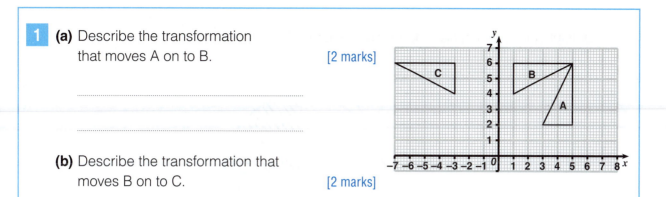

2 Describe fully the single transformation
that maps P on to Q. [3 marks]

....

....

....

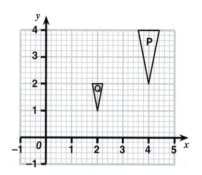

3 (a) Plot the triangle T with coordinates
(3, 3), (3, 1) and (4, 1). [1 mark]

(b) Rotate T 90° clockwise with centre
(0, 0) and label the image V. [2 marks]

(c) Reflect V in the y-axis and label the
image W. [2 marks]

(d) What transformation maps V back
on to T? [2 marks]

....

....

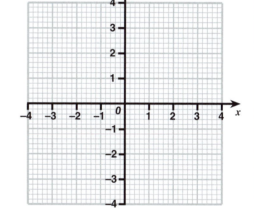

4 Enlarge this shape with:

(a) scale factor 2, centre (3, 5) [2 marks]

(b) scale factor 0.5, centre (0, 0) [2 marks]

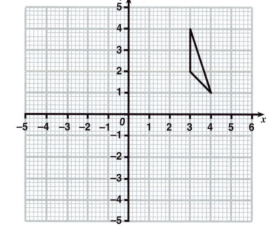

Score /18

For more help on this topic, see Letts GCSE Maths Foundation Revision Guide pages 64–65.

Module 28

1 Complete the following statements with the correct word.

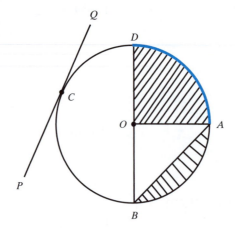

(a) *OA* is the _____ of the circle. [1 mark]

(b) *BD* is a _____. [1 mark]

(c) *PCQ* is a _____ to the circle at *C*. [1 mark]

(d) The curved line around the full circle is the _____. [1 mark]

(e) The blue line *AD* is an _____. [1 mark]

(f) The shaded area *OAD* is a _____. [1 mark]

(g) The shaded area between *A* and *B* is a _____. [1 mark]

(h) *OAB* is an _____ triangle. [1 mark]

2 Calculate the circumference of this circle. Give your answer to 2 significant figures. [3 marks]

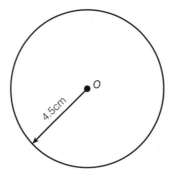

_____ cm

3 Calculate the area of a circle with diameter 8cm. Give your answer in terms of π. ⊘ [3 marks]

....

4 What is the perimeter of this shape? [2 marks]

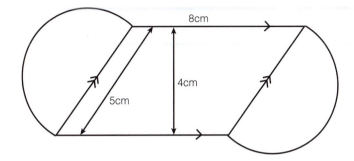

.... cm

5 This is the net for a cone.

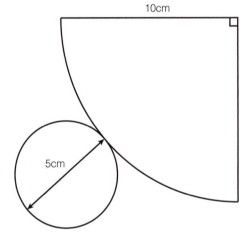

Calculate the surface area. [4 marks]

....

6 A plane circles the Earth at an altitude of 11km.

If the radius of the Earth is 6370km, how much further does the plane travel than someone making the same journey at sea-level? [3 marks]

.... km

Score   **/23**

For more help on this topic, see Letts GCSE Maths Foundation Revision Guide pages 66–67.

1 What 3D shape has 6 faces, 10 edges and 6 vertices? [2 marks]

....

2 Sketch two different 3D solids with five faces and name them. [3 marks]

3 Draw the plan and elevations of this 3D shape. [4 marks]

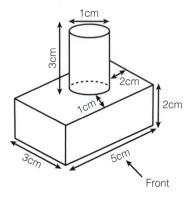

4 Sketch the 3D shape shown by this plan and elevations. [3 marks]

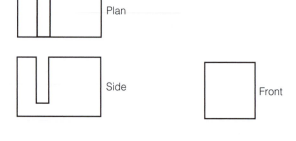

Plan

Side

Front

Score /12

For more help on this topic, see Letts GCSE Maths Foundation Revision Guide pages 68–69.

1 Calculate the area and perimeter of these shapes.

(a)
[3 marks]

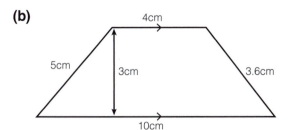

Area: .... m²

Perimeter: .... m

(b)
[3 marks]

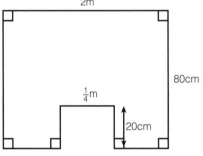

Area: .... cm²

Perimeter: .... cm

2 Calculate the area of this shape.
[2 marks]

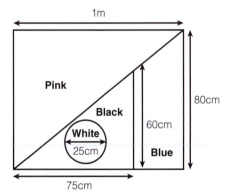

....

3 Look at this design for a flag.

Pink

Black

White
25cm

Blue

1m

80cm

60cm

75cm

Calculate the area of this flag that is:

(a) pink
[2 marks]

....

(b) blue
[2 marks]

....

(c) black
[2 marks]

....

4 Calculate the surface area of a cylinder with radius 4cm and height 5cm.
Give your answer in terms of π.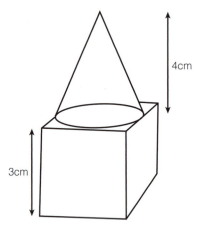

[3 marks]

.... cm²

5 This shape is a cone of vertical height 4cm sitting on a cube of side 3cm.
Calculate its volume.

[3 marks]

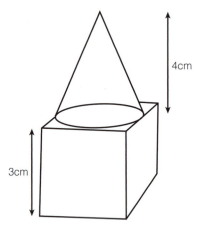

4cm

3cm

....

6 A sphere of radius 3.5cm and a cube with sides a cm have the same volume.

Find a. Give your answer to 3 significant figures.

[3 marks]

.... cm

7 Calculate the volume of a hemisphere with radius 5cm.
Give your answer in terms of π.

[3 marks]

....

8 Which has the larger surface area, a cuboid
with dimensions 4.4cm × 5.3cm × 1.8cm
or a hemisphere with radius 2.8cm?

[4 marks]

....

Score **/30**

For more help on this topic, see Letts GCSE Maths Foundation Revision Guide pages 70–71.

Module 31

Perimeter, Area and Volume

1 (a) Work out the size of angle *p*. [3 marks]

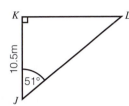

2.8cm
3.5cm

(b) Find the length *KL*. Give your answer to 3 significant figures. [3 marks]

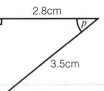

K *L*
10.5m
51°
J

.... m

2 (a) Calculate the length *NP*. [2 marks]

(b) Find angle *NOP*. [3 marks]

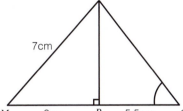

N
7cm
M 6cm *P* 5.5cm *O*

3 Find *q*, leaving your answer as a square root. [3 marks]

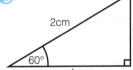

7cm
*q*cm
9cm

4 (a) Write down the value of:

    (i) sin 45° [1 mark]

    (ii) tan 45° [1 mark]

(b) Calculate *a* and *b*. [4 marks]

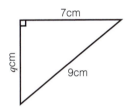

2cm
a
60°
b

a = ...

b = ...

5 A builder uses a ramp to push his wheelbarrow on to a platform.

If the platform is 1m high and the ramp is 5m long, what angle does the ramp make with the ground? [3 marks]

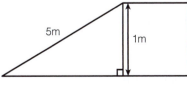

5m
1m

Score /23

For more help on this topic, see Letts GCSE Maths Foundation Revision Guide pages 72–73.

1 Here are base vectors **r**, **s** and **t** drawn on isometric paper.

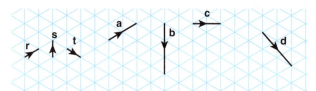

Write each of the vectors **a** to **d** in terms of **r**, **s** and **t**.   [4 marks]

a = ...   **b** = ...   **c** = ...   **d** = ...

2 OPQRST is a regular hexagon. X is the midpoint of QR.

$\overrightarrow{OP}$ = **a**, $\overrightarrow{OT}$ = **b** and $\overrightarrow{PQ}$ = **c**.

Write the following vectors in terms of **a**, **b** and **c**.

(a) $\overrightarrow{QR}$ ....   [1 mark]

(b) $\overrightarrow{RQ}$ ....   [1 mark]

(c) $\overrightarrow{OQ}$ ....   [1 mark]

(d) $\overrightarrow{SQ}$ ....   [1 mark]

(e) $\overrightarrow{QT}$ ....   [1 mark]

(f) $\overrightarrow{TX}$ ....   [1 mark]

3 ABCD is a parallelogram.
BE is a straight line with AB = AE.
$\overrightarrow{AB}$ = **b** and $\overrightarrow{AD}$ = **d**.

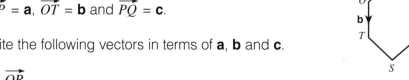

(a) Write $\overrightarrow{BE}$ in terms of **b** and **d**.   ....   [1 mark]

(b) Write $\overrightarrow{AC}$ in terms of **b** and **d**.   ....   [2 marks]

(c) Write $\overrightarrow{CE}$ in terms of **b** and **d**.   ....   [2 marks]

4 PQR is an equilateral triangle.
OPQ is an isosceles triangle with OQ = PQ
$\overrightarrow{OQ}$ = **q** and $\overrightarrow{OP}$ = **p**.

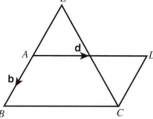

Find $\overrightarrow{OR}$, $\overrightarrow{PQ}$ and $\overrightarrow{PR}$.   [3 marks]

$\overrightarrow{OR}$ = ... $\overrightarrow{PQ}$ = ... $\overrightarrow{PR}$ = ...

Score   /18

For more help on this topic, see Letts GCSE Maths Foundation Revision Guide pages 74–75.

1 A fair dice is rolled. Mark on the probability scale the probability of rolling:

(a) an odd number, P(odd) [1 mark]

(b) a 5 or a 6, P(5 or 6) [1 mark]

(c) a 7, P(7) [1 mark]

```
├──────┬──────┬──────┬──────┬──────┬──────┤
0              0.5                  1
```

2 There are three bananas, five oranges, four apples and two mangoes in a fruit bowl. A piece of fruit is taken at random.

Find the probability that it is:

(a) an apple .... [1 mark]

(b) a banana or a mango .... [1 mark]

(c) not an orange .... [1 mark]

3 The table shows the probability that Mark will choose a certain activity when he gets home from school on any given day.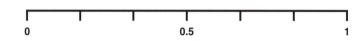

Activity	Watch TV	Do homework	Play on computer	Go for a bike ride	Other
Probability	0.2		0.3	0.25	0.1

Find the probability that Mark will do homework on any given day. [2 marks]

....

4 Brian bought a dice from the joke shop. He rolled it 25 times and recorded the results. Here are the results:

Number	1	2	3	4	5	6
Frequency	0	3	2	4	4	12

(a) Find the relative frequency of rolling a 6. [1 mark]

....

Brian rolls the dice another 250 times.

(b) How many times would he be expected to get an even number? [3 marks]

....

Score /12

For more help on this topic, see Letts GCSE Maths Foundation Revision Guide pages 78–79.

1 A fair dice and a coin are thrown at the same time.

List all the possible outcomes. The first one is done for you. [2 marks]

(1, head) ....

....

2 A fair dice is thrown and a spinner is spun. The spinner has three equal sides – one side marked 1, a second side marked 3 and a third side marked 5. The scores on the dice and spinner are added together.

(a) Draw a sample space diagram to show all the possible outcomes. [2 marks]

(b) What is the probability of getting a score higher than 7? [1 mark]

....

(c) Find the probability of scoring an even number. [1 mark]

....

3 Fifty students are invited to vote for a new class president. They can each vote for a maximum of two people from Luke (L), Dan (D) and Jack (J).

Luke gets 26 votes altogether
7 students vote for Dan and Luke
2 students vote for Dan and Jack

Dan gets 17 votes altogether
4 students vote for Luke and Jack
3 students don't vote

(a) Complete the Venn diagram to show this information. The universal set ε contains all 50 students. [3 marks]

ε

L   D

J

(b) Find the probability that a student chosen at random votes for Jack only. [1 mark]

....

Score   /10

For more help on this topic, see Letts GCSE Maths Foundation Revision Guide pages 80–81.

1 A washing powder manufacturer conducts a survey of the actual weight of powder in the 500g boxes on the production line.

A sample of 12 boxes is taken over a period of 1 hour:

495, 503, 490, 505, 490, 498, 500, 510, 505, 498, 498, 501

(a) What is the mode for the sample? [1 mark]

....

(b) Find the median. [1 mark]

....

(c) The manufacturer produces 10 000 boxes per hour.
Give two reasons why this may not be a good sample. [2 marks]

....

....

2 The table shows the weights of 160 different species of birds in a forest.

Weight (g)	Frequency
$30 \leqslant w < 40$	20
$40 \leqslant w < 50$	25
$50 \leqslant w < 60$	22
$60 \leqslant w < 80$	44
$80 \leqslant w < 100$	32
$100 \leqslant w < 120$	15
$120 \leqslant w < 150$	2
	160

(a) Which class interval contains the median? [1 mark]

....

(b) Calculate an estimate of the mean weight of the birds. [3 marks]

....

(c) What percentage of the birds weigh less than 80g? [2 marks]

....

3 There are five cards with an integer on each. The mean of all the numbers on the cards is 7. Both the mode and the median of the numbers are 6.

What numbers could be on the cards? 📝 [3 marks]

....

Score /13

For more help on this topic, see Letts GCSE Maths Foundation Revision Guide pages 84–85.

Module 36

1 The table shows the sales figures for a car dealership over two different weeks.

(a) There were 100 car sales in total in week 2.
Complete the table. [1 mark]

(b) Show this data in a suitable chart. [3 marks]

Sales	Week 1	Week 2
Monday	10	25
Tuesday	25	20
Wednesday	29	15
Thursday	40	19
Friday	16	

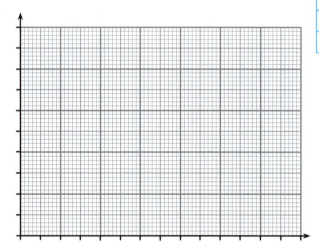

2 Sixty cat owners were asked about which treats they buy for their cats:

• 35 said they bought Biscuit Treats

• 19 said they bought Meaty Sticks

• 14 owners said they bought both products

Complete the Venn diagram. [3 marks]

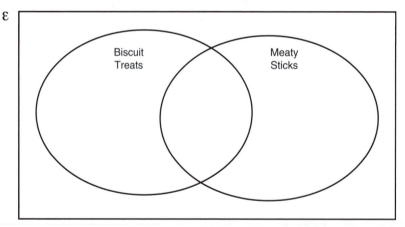

3 The manager of a pizza shop conducts a survey of favourite pizzas. She wants to show this information on a pie chart.

	Frequency	Angle
Vegetarian	45	60°
Seafood	80	
Meat	50	
Chicken	40	
Mushroom		

Complete the table. [2 marks]

4 The table shows the sales of a particular type of mobile phone over an eight-year period.

Year	1	2	3	4	5	6	7	8
Sales (millions)	2	10	20	40	70	125	150	170

(a) By plotting a suitable graph, use this information to predict the sales for year 9.   [3 marks]

....

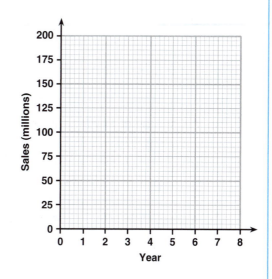

(b) Comment on the reliability of using your graph to predict sales in year 14.   [2 marks]

....

....

5 The speeds of 12 drivers and their ages were recorded in the table below. John says that 'younger drivers drive too fast'.

Age (years)	20	32	24	30	22	40	35	34	42	22	38	32
Speed (mph)	38	30	37	32	39	30	32	33	28	36	27	34

(a) Use an appropriate diagram to comment on whether the data supports John's conclusion.   [3 marks]

....

....

....

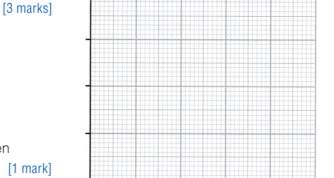

(b) Describe the relationship between age and driving speed.   [1 mark]

....

....

Score   /18

For more help on this topic, see Letts GCSE Maths Foundation Revision Guide pages 86–87.

Statistical Diagrams

Module 37

1 Complete the table with a tick (✓) or a cross (✗). The first row has been completed for you.

[2 marks]

	Represents a single value	Affected by outliers	Measure of spread
Mode	✓	✗	✗
Median			
Mean			
Range			

2 The test scores of 24 students in a history exam are given below.

Class A	33	45	67	83	56	23	57	45	73	43	26	35
Class B	33	27	40	44	78	28	49	38	54	32	51	74

Which class did better? Give reasons for your answer. [5 marks]

....

....

....

....

....

....

3 Claire surveys 40 members of her running club to find out how far they run every week.

She analyses her results and calculates the mean as 8.5 miles and the median as 7 miles. She then decides to include her own distance of 9 miles. 🖩

(a) The new mean is: [1 mark]

Lower ☐   No different ☐   Higher ☐

Reason: ....

....

(b) What will be the effect on the median once Claire's distance is included in the results? [1 mark]

....

....

4 The tables below show the results of a survey on the cost of car insurance for 30–50 year olds and for under 30 year olds.

30–50 year olds

Cost (£)	Frequency		
$100 \leqslant c < 150$	10		
$150 \leqslant c < 200$	38		
$200 \leqslant c < 250$	48		
$250 \leqslant c < 300$	31		
$300 \leqslant c < 350$	20		
$350 \leqslant c < 400$	8		
$400 \leqslant c < 500$	5		

Under 30s

Cost (£)	Frequency		
$100 \leqslant c < 150$	2		
$150 \leqslant c < 200$	15		
$200 \leqslant c < 250$	10		
$250 \leqslant c < 300$	21		
$300 \leqslant c < 350$	42		
$350 \leqslant c < 400$	45		
$400 \leqslant c < 500$	25		

Compare the cost of insurance for the two sets of drivers. [5 marks]

Comparison 1: ....

....

....

Comparison 2: ....

....

....

Score /14

For more help on this topic, see Letts GCSE Maths Foundation Revision Guide pages 88–89.

Comparing Distributions **Module 38** 49

Module 38

GCSE
Mathematics
Foundation tier

Paper 1   Time: 1 hour 30 minutes

For this paper you must have:

- mathematical instruments

You must **not** use a calculator.

Instructions

- Use black ink or black ball-point pen. Draw diagrams in pencil.
- Read each question carefully before you start to write your answer.
- Diagrams are not accurately drawn unless otherwise stated.
- Answer **all** the questions.
- Answer the questions in the space provided.
- In all calculations, show clearly how you work out your answer. Use a separate sheet of paper if needed. Marks may be given for a correct method even if the answer is wrong.

Information

- The mark for each question is shown in brackets.
- The maximum mark for this paper is 80.

Name: ....

1. **(a)** Work out

   $20 + 3 \times 2$ [1]

   ....

   (b) Write 30% as a decimal. [1]

   ....

   (c) Write 0.15 as a fraction in its simplest form. [2]

   ....

2. Which average is affected most by an outlier? [1]

   ....

3. A bag contains three green counters, two blue counters and one white counter.
A counter is taken at random.

Draw and label arrows on the probability scale to show the probability of:

- Picking a green counter (G)

- Picking a blue counter (B)

- Picking a pink counter (P)   [2]

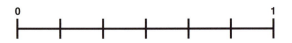

4. Dorcas is thinking of a number. She multiplies it by 4 and then adds 3. She gets the answer –5.

What number was she thinking of?   [2]

5. The results of a survey on the lifetime (in hours) of two different light bulbs are shown in the table.

	Magnabulb	Lighthouse Bulbs
Estimated mean	355	380
Median	340	365
Range	88	132

(a) Give one reason why Lighthouse Bulbs might be better.   [1]

(b) Give one reason why Magnabulb might be better.   [1]

6. Write down all the factors of 40. [2]

....

7. **(a)** Write down the value of 3^3. [1]

....

(b) Write down the value of 10^4. [1]

....

(c) Write down the value of $\sqrt[3]{8}$. [1]

....

8. Work out

$$\frac{3}{5}+\frac{1}{4}$$ [2]

....

9. George, Timmy and Ann shared some money in the ratio 5 : 7 : 9

Ann got £32 more than Timmy.

How much money did George get? [3]

£ ....

10. Jenni plays violin in an orchestra. She has 22 performances this year. For each performance she needs to get a return train ticket which costs £8.85. The orchestra pays $\frac{1}{4}$ of her travel costs.

(a) Estimate how much Jenni will have to pay in travel costs for the year. **[2]**

£ ....

(b) Calculate the exact cost of the train tickets for the year. **[2]**

£ ....

11. Solve the simultaneous equations $4x + y = 1$ **[4]**

$2x - y = 5$

$x =$ .... $y =$ ....

12. There are some orange and mint chocolates in a bag.

The probability of taking a mint chocolate is $\frac{1}{3}$

Amorreane takes a mint chocolate at random and eats it.

The probability of taking a mint chocolate is now $\frac{1}{4}$

How many orange chocolates are in the bag? [2]

....

13. Increase £340 by 15% [2]

....

14. A fair four-sided dice has the following coloured sides – blue, green, white and red.

The dice is rolled twice.

Complete the table to show all of the possible outcomes. [2]

		Second roll			
		Blue	**Green**	**White**	**Red**
First roll	**Blue**	B, B	B, G		
	Green	G, B			
	White				
	Red				

15. Ketsia starts with the number 3. She takes away a and then multiplies by b.

She gets an answer of 28. a is a negative integer and b is a positive integer.

Find two possible pairs of values for a and b.   **[2]**

$a =$ .... $b =$ ....

$a =$ .... $b =$ ....

16. Work out

$$\frac{5}{8} \div \frac{2}{3}$$ **[1]**

....

17.

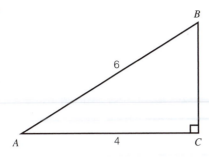

(a) Write down the value of cos A. **[1]**

....

(b) Calculate the length of BC. Leave your answer as a square root. **[3]**

....

18. Solve the equation $(x+1)(x-9)=0$ **[2]**

$x =$ .... or $x =$ ....

19. Alfred is 14 years old, Bertha is 15 and Cedric is 21. Every year they share £1400 in the ratio of their ages.

(a) How much money does Bertha get this year? **[2]**

....

(b) Does Cedric get more or less in two years' time? Show working to support your answer. **[3]**

....

20. Simplify $\left(3x^2y^5\right)^2$ [2]

....

21. The total TV sales over a five-year period for a national electrical store were 120 000 units.

Find the sales figures for computers and TVs in year 4. [3]

Year	Computer sales (thousands)	TV sales (thousands)
1	12	
2	14	
3	13	
4	a	$2a + 5$
5	16	

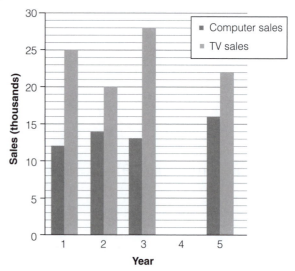

TV sales: ....

Computer sales: ....

22. Find the equation of the line that is parallel to $y = 2x + 7$ and passes through the point $(0, -3)$. [2]

....

23. Here is a square and an isosceles triangle.

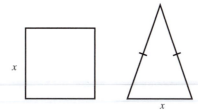

The length of each of the equal sides of the triangle is 3cm greater than the side of the square.

(a) If the perimeters of the two shapes are equal, find the value of x. **[3]**

....

(b) Show that the height of the triangle is equal to the diagonal of the square. **[3]**

....

....

....

....

24. Calculate the circumference of this circle.

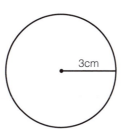

3cm

Leave your answer in terms of π. **[2]**

.... cm

25. Which is more, 15% of 260 or 18% of 210?

Show your working. **[3]**

....

26. The fastest land animal is the **cheetah**, which has a recorded speed of 75mph.

The **peregrine falcon** is the fastest bird, with a speed of 389km/h.

The fastest animal in the sea is the **black marlin**, which has a recorded speed of 36m/s.

Put the speeds of these animals in order, fastest first. 5 miles = 8 kilometres **[3]**

....

27. Two cones S and T have volumes of 240cm³ and 810cm³ respectively.

(a) Write the ratio of the volumes S : T in its simplest form. **[1]**

....

(b) What is the ratio of the heights S : T? **[1]**

....

(c) If the surface area of cone S is 180cm², what is the surface area of cone T? **[2]**

.... cm²

28. The diagram below shows the graph of $y = x^2 - 8x + 17$

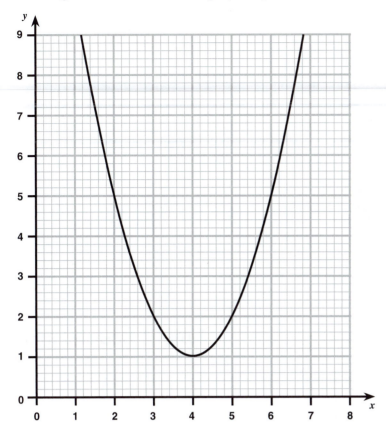

(a) Write down the equation of the line of symmetry. [2]

....

(b) Write down the coordinates of the turning point on the curve. [2]

....

(c) If the graph was extended, at which coordinates would it cross the y-axis? [2]

....

GCSE
Mathematics
Foundation tier

Paper 2   Time: 1 hour 30 minutes

For this paper you must have:

- a calculator
- mathematical instruments

Instructions

- Use black ink or black ball-point pen. Draw diagrams in pencil.
- Read each question carefully before you start to write your answer.
- Diagrams are not accurately drawn unless otherwise stated.
- Answer **all** the questions.
- Answer the questions in the space provided.
- In all calculations, show clearly how you work out your answer. Use a separate sheet of paper if needed. Marks may be given for a correct method even if the answer is wrong.
- If your calculator does not have a π button, take the value of π to be 3.142 unless the question instructs otherwise.

Information

- The mark for each question is shown in brackets.
- The maximum mark for this paper is 80.

Name: ....

1. Here are some numbers:

| 7 | 4 | 9 | 42 | 28 | 56 |

From this list of numbers write down:

(a) A multiple of 6 [1]

....

(b) A factor of 45 [1]

....

(c) A prime number [1]

....

2. Find the value of:

(a) 2.7^3 [1]

....

(b) $\sqrt{576}$ [1]

....

(c) $\sqrt[3]{9261}$ [1]

....

3. Match each speed–time graph, A, B and C, to the correct distance–time graph. **[2]**

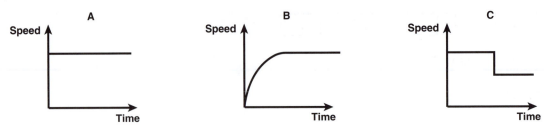

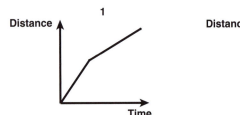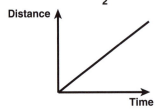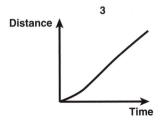

4. Lela is buying some new stationery. She buys:

- Three gel pens at £1.19 each
- Two erasers at 17p each
- Four pencils at 26p each
- A ruler at 45p

Lela pays with a £10 note.

How much change does she receive? **[3]**

5. Find two numbers, **greater than 71**, which have the following **two** properties:

- a multiple of 5 and 7
- a common factor of 420 and 630 **[4]**

6. Expand

(a) $6(x - 3)$ [2]

....

(b) $(x + 3)(x - 3)$ [2]

....

7. Calculate the area of this shape. Give your answer to 3 significant figures. [3]

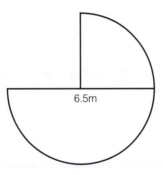

6.5m

....

8. A biologist conducted a survey of different lakes to investigate algae growth and the amounts of nitrate present. She recorded the concentrations of both algae and nitrate in a table.

Algae (cells/ml)	10	12	55	20	5	24	42	44	15	30	22	38
Nitrate (mg/L)	0.5	1.5	3.6	0.7	0.5	1.8	1.5	1.8	1.7	2.3	0.8	2.6

(a) Draw a scatter graph of this data on the grid below. [2]

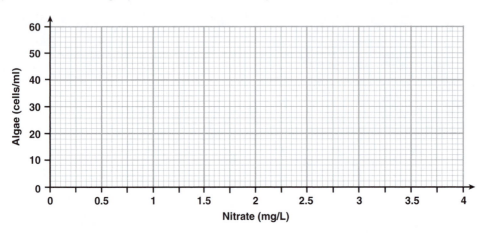

(b) What type of correlation is shown between nitrate levels and algae concentrations? [1]

....

(c) Use the graph to estimate the nitrate levels in a lake with an algae concentration of 28 cells/ml. [2]

.... mg/L

(d) The biologist wants to use this data to predict algae concentrations for any lake.

Comment on the biologist's idea. [1]

....

....

9. **(a)** Work out the following. Write down all the figures on your calculator display. [2]

$$\frac{\sqrt{35} + 6^2}{(2 - 0.04)^3}$$

....

(b) Round your answer in part (a) to 3 significant figures. [1]

....

10. Show that the point $(-3, -2)$ lies on the curve $y = x^2 + 2x - 5$ [2]

....

....

....

....

11. Three feeding bowls, A, B and C, are placed in a cage with two hamsters. The hamsters are equally likely to choose any of the feeding bowls.

Find the probability that both hamsters choose bowl C. [2]

....

12. The following shape is made up of equilateral triangles.

Shade exactly $\frac{11}{16}$ of the shape. [2]

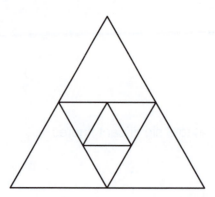

13. The distance from London to Manchester is 200 miles to the nearest 10 miles.

(a) What is the shortest possible distance, in miles, between London and Manchester? [1]

....

(b) Write down the error interval for the distance (d) between London and Manchester. [1]

....

14. The nth term in an arithmetic sequence is given by $U_n = 5n + 2$

Write down the first four terms in this sequence. [2]

....

15. Matthew is estimating the height of his house using the Sun.

A stick 1m long casts a shadow 60cm long. At the same time the shadow of the house is 5.4m long.

How tall is the house? **[3]**

....

16. Jerome is a salesman. He visits farms to try to sell gates and fencing equipment.

When Jerome visits a farm, the probability that he will make a sale is 0.4

One morning Jerome visits two farms.

(a) Complete the tree diagram to show all the outcomes. **[2]**

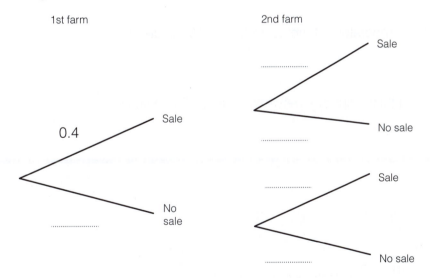

(b) Find the probability that Jerome sells equipment to at least one of the farms. **[2]**

....

17. The graph shows the temperature of a jug of custard as it cools.

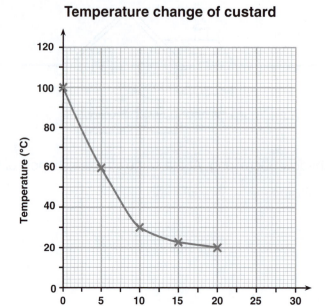

Temperature change of custard

(a) Describe what happens in the first 5 minutes. [2]

....

....

....

....

(b) What is the temperature of the custard after 15 minutes? [1]

....

(c) What do you think happens between 20 and 30 minutes? [2]

....

....

....

....

18. Rearrange $y = \dfrac{10x - 2}{5 - x}$ to make x the subject. [4]

....

19. Calculate the surface area of this cylinder. Give your answer to 3 significant figures.   **[3]**

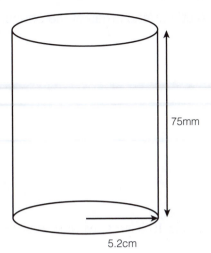

75mm

5.2cm

.... cm²

20. Calculate the angle R. Give your answer to 3 significant figures.   **[3]**

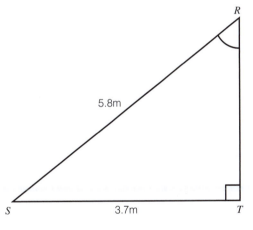

R

5.8m

S 3.7m T

....

21. The ratio of the radii of two cones is 1 : 3

(a) Calculate the ratio of the curved surface areas of the cones. [1]

....

(b) If the volume of the larger cone is 10.8 litres, what is the volume of the smaller cone? [2]

....

22. Work out the equation of the line that is parallel to the line $y = 7 - 2x$ and passes through the point (8, −1). [4]

....

23. Copper and zinc are mixed to form an alloy in the ratio 9 : 7 by mass.

(a) If 27kg of copper are used to make a batch of alloy, how much alloy can be made? **[3]**

.... kg

(b) The density of copper is 8900kg/m³.

Find its density in g/cm³. **[4]**

.... g/cm³

24. Calculate angle *BCD*, giving your reasons. **[3]**

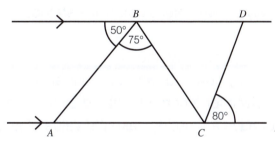

....

....

....

....

GCSE
Mathematics
Foundation tier

Paper 3

Time: 1 hour 30 minutes

For this paper you must have:

- a calculator
- mathematical instruments

Instructions

- Use black ink or black ball-point pen. Draw diagrams in pencil.
- Read each question carefully before you start to write your answer.
- Diagrams are not accurately drawn unless otherwise stated.
- Answer **all** the questions.
- Answer the questions in the space provided.
- In all calculations, show clearly how you work out your answer. Use a separate sheet of paper if needed. Marks may be given for a correct method even if the answer is wrong.
- If your calculator does not have a π button, take the value of π to be 3.142 unless the question instructs otherwise.

Information

- The mark for each question is shown in brackets.
- The maximum mark for this paper is 80.

Name: ....

1. Shade $\frac{2}{3}$ of this shape.   [1]

2. Write the following numbers in order from smallest to largest.

    (a) −5   3   7   −7   −3   0   [1]

    ....

    (b) 0.39   0.33   0.03   0.3   0.309   [1]

    ....

3. **(a)** Round 345.934 to 2 significant figures.   [1]

    ....

    (b) Round 0.30492 to 3 significant figures.   [1]

    ....

4. (a) Write the number 180 as a product of its prime factors. [2]

....

(b) Write your answer to part (a) in index form. [1]

....

5. Twenty-five pensioners are asked if they like tea or coffee. These are the responses:

- 18 like tea
- 19 like coffee
- 4 like tea but not coffee

Draw a Venn diagram to display these results. [3]

6. A restaurant has this special offer:

- £2.95 for a starter

- £6.50 for a main course

- £2.25 for a dessert

How much do two people pay in total if they each have three courses? **[2]**

£ ....

7. Water is poured into each of the containers A, B and C at a constant rate. The graphs show how the depth of water changes (*y*-axis) with time (*x*-axis).

Match each container with its correct graph. **[2]**

A

B

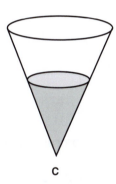

C

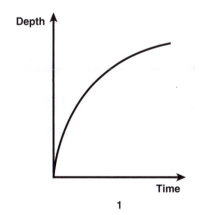

1

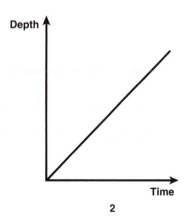

2

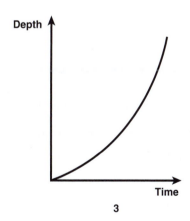

3

8. Lee weighs 89.3kg to the nearest 1 decimal place.

(a) What is the least amount that Lee could weigh? **[1]**

.... kg

(b) Write down the error interval for Lee's weight (W). **[2]**

....

9. A new tablet computer is released and the older model costing £425 is reduced by 12%.

What is its new price? **[2]**

£ ....

10. James pays £6 and Jamila pays £4 towards a raffle ticket. The ticket wins the star prize of £80.

If they share the money in the same ratio as they paid originally, how much more money does James get? **[3]**

....

11. Lyse and Lysette each test out a biased coin to find out the estimated probability of it landing on heads. Here are the results:

	Number of coin flips	Number of heads
Lyse	40	16
Lysette	80	28

(a) Whose results give the best estimate for the probability of getting heads?

Explain your answer. [1]

....

....

....

....

The coin is flipped 600 times.

(b) How many times do you expect the coin to land on heads? [2]

....

12. Find an integer value of x satisfying both $3x + 4 > 19$ and $2x - 1 < 13$ [3]

....

13. Sketch two graphs to show:

(a) y directly proportional to x. [2]

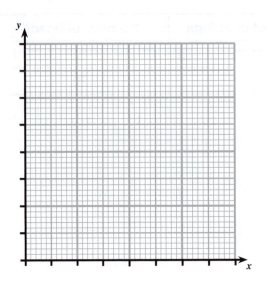

(b) y inversely proportional to x. [2]

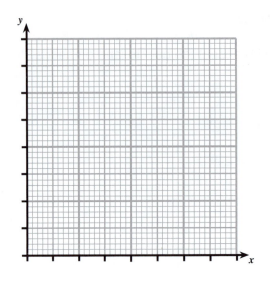

14. (a) Write $3^5 \div 3^{10}$ as a single power of 3. [1]

....

(b) Write $0.000\,070\,2$ in standard form. [1]

....

(c) Calculate the value of 6^{-2} [1]

....

15. Here is a map of part of Norway.

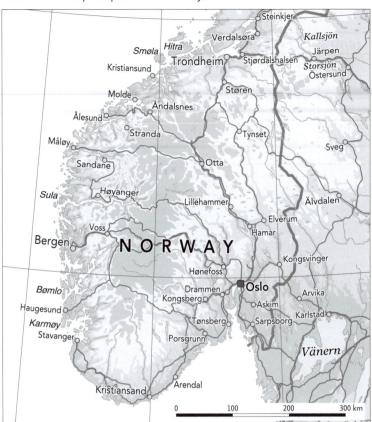

Scale 1 : 6 500 000

(a) Estimate the straight-line distance from Trondheim to Bergen. **[2]**

....

(b) The actual road and ferry journey is 700km.

Express the road and ferry distance as a percentage of the straight-line distance. **[2]**

....

(c) If it takes 11 hours to make the journey by car, what is the average speed? **[3]**

....

16. A farmer measures the growth (measured as a change in height) of his crop over a period of eight weeks. The results are shown in the table below.

Growth (cm)	Frequency
$0 \leqslant h < 20$	11
$20 \leqslant h < 40$	38
$40 \leqslant h < 60$	49
$60 \leqslant h < 80$	30
$80 \leqslant h < 120$	12

(a) Which is the modal group? [1]

....

(b) Find the estimated mean growth for the crop over this period. [3]

.... cm

(c) The farmer says that over one-third of his crop grew by 60cm or more during this period.

Does the data support the farmer's claim? [2]

....

....

....

....

....

17. Using algebra, solve the equation $x^2 + 6x - 27 = 0$ [4]

....

18. The International Space Station (ISS) travels at a speed of 4.48×10^4 km/h.

(a) Write this value as an ordinary number. [1]

....

It takes three hours for the ISS to orbit the Earth twice.

(b) Find the distance that the ISS travels in one full orbit around the Earth.

Write your answer in standard form. [3]

....

19. Consider the function $f(x) = \dfrac{3x + 9}{2}$

(a) Write down the outputs for each of the following inputs: [4]

Input x   **Output $f(x)$**

0                    $\rightarrow$ ....

1                    $\rightarrow$ ....

2                    $\rightarrow$ ....

3                    $\rightarrow$ ....

(b) Find the value of x that maps to itself. [2]

....

20.

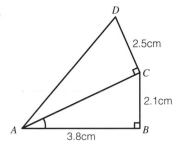

Find

(a) The size of angle CAB. [2]

....

(b) The area of triangle ACD. [4]

....

21. The value of a motorbike (£V) is given by the formula $V = 18\,000 \times 0.85^t$ where t is the age in whole number of years.

(a) What is the value of the bike when it is new? [1]

....

(b) What is the bike worth after two years? [2]

....

(c) After how many years will its value be below £10 000? [2]

....

22. Look at shape A on this grid.

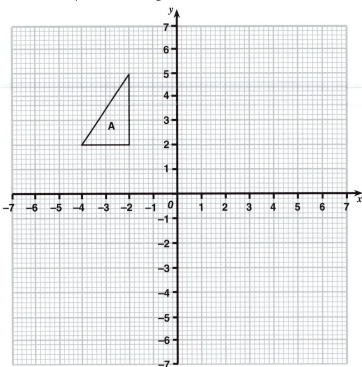

(a) Rotate shape A through 180° about centre (1, 0). Label the shape B. **[2]**

(b) Reflect shape B in the x-axis and label the new shape C. **[2]**

(c) Enlarge shape A, scale factor 2, centre (−6, 6). Label the enlarged shape D. **[2]**

Notes

Module 1: Place Value and Ordering

1. **(a)** −7 **(b)** 21 **(c)** −3

   Remember the rules for signs and BIDMAS.

2. **(a)** False **(b)** True **(c)** True **(d)** False
3. **(a)** −3°C **(b)** −9°C
4. **(a)** 5.418 **(b)** 5418 **(c)** 12 900 **(d)** 420

   Compare the position of decimal points with the original calculation.

5. **(a)** £35 [Accept −£35]
   (b) £35 − £14 [1] = £21 [1] [Accept −£21]

Module 2: Factors, Multiples and Primes

1. **(a)** 1 and 3 **(b)** 1, 4 and 16 **(c)** 6, 12, 24 and 48
2. 21 [1] or 45 [1]

   Test the prime numbers between 1 and 50.

3. **(a)** 55 **(b)** 7
4. **(a)** $72 = 2 \times 2 \times 18 = 2 \times 2 \times 2 \times 3 \times 3$ [2] [Two correct steps of decomposition get 1 mark] $= 2^3 \times 3^2$ [1]

   Use factor trees.

   (b) $90 = 2 \times 3 \times 15$ [1] $= 2 \times 3 \times 3 \times 5$ [1] $= 2 \times 3^2 \times 5$ [1]
   (c) $2 \times 3 \times 3$ [1] $= 18$ [1]

   Look for the common factors from the lists in (a) and (b).

   (d) $18 \times 2 \times 2 \times 5$ [1] $= 360$ [1]

   HCF × remaining factors.

5. Bus A: 12 24 36 48 60 72 84
   Bus B: 28 56 84 112 140 168 196 [1]
   LCM = 84 [1]
   8.00am + 84 minutes = 9.24am [1]

Module 3: Operations

1. **(a)** 17

   Multiplication before addition.

   (b) $\dfrac{3}{5}$

   (c) $\dfrac{1}{4}$

2. $\dfrac{(2)^2}{2}$ [1] $= 2$ [1]

3. **(a)** $\dfrac{12}{40}$ [1] $= \dfrac{3}{10}$ [1]   **(b)** $\dfrac{50}{18}$ [1] $= 2\dfrac{7}{9}$ [1]

   Find the reciprocal of the second fraction and multiply.

   (c) $\dfrac{15-12}{20}$ [1] $= \dfrac{3}{20}$ [1]   **(d)** $\dfrac{9+5}{15}$ [1] $= \dfrac{14}{15}$ [1]

   Find a common denominator.

4. $1 - \left(\dfrac{2}{5} + \dfrac{3}{7}\right)$ [1] $= 1 - \dfrac{29}{35}$ [1] $= \dfrac{6}{35}$ [1]

5. $1\dfrac{1}{4} \times 2\dfrac{2}{3}$ [1] $= \dfrac{5}{4} \times \dfrac{8}{3}$ [1] $= \dfrac{40}{12} = 3\dfrac{1}{3}\text{m}^2$ [1]

6. $1 - \left(\dfrac{3}{5} + \dfrac{2}{9}\right)$ [1] $= 1 - \dfrac{37}{45}$ [1] $= \dfrac{8}{45}$ [1]

Module 4: Powers and Roots

1. **(a)** 3^6 **(b)** 12^4

2. $\sqrt[3]{64}$ $\sqrt[4]{625}$ 5^2 3^3 2^5

3. **(a)** $x = 7$ **(b)** $x = 125$ **(c)** $x = 3$

4. **(a)** 4^2

   Subtract the powers, i.e. 4^{6-4}

   (b) 5^{-2}
   (c) 0.0003

   The digits have moved four places.

5. **(a) (i)** 3.21×10^5 **(ii)** 6.05×10^{-4}
   (b) (i) 30×10^{-5} [1] $= 3 \times 10^{-4}$ [1]
   (ii) $41\,000 + 3400 = 44\,400$ [1] $= 4.44 \times 10^4$ [1]

6. **(a)** 1 **(b)** $\dfrac{1}{4^2} = \dfrac{1}{16}$

Module 5: Fractions, Decimals and Percentages

1. **(a)** 0.7
   (b) 0.75
   (c) 0.36

2. $\dfrac{17}{51}$ $\dfrac{3}{8}$ 0.475 $\dfrac{12}{25}$

   Convert all the values to decimals to compare them.

3. $\dfrac{56}{100} = \dfrac{14}{25}$

4. $5 \div 8 = 0.625$ [1] $7 \div 11 = 0.6363...$ [1]

   $\dfrac{7}{11}$ is closer to $\dfrac{2}{3}$ (as $\dfrac{2}{3} = 0.6666...$) [1]

5. **(a)** $37 \times 49 = 1813$ [1]
   So $3.7 \times 4.9 = 18.13$ [1]
   (b) $560 \div 14$ [1] $= 40$
   So $56 \div 1.4 = 40$ [1]

6. 34×129 [1] $= 4386$ [1]
   So total cost is £43.86 [1]

   Use long multiplication.

7. 0.2222...

   Use long division.

Module 6: Approximations

1. **(a)** 3500 **(b)** 29 **(c)** 700
2. **(a)** 9.49 **(b)** 6.554 **(c)** 5.60

   Use a calculator first.

3. **(a)** 400 000 **(b)** 0.0497 **(c)** 3.142

   Use a calculator to find π.

4. $\dfrac{20 \times 3}{0.5} = \dfrac{60}{0.5} = 120$ [2]
   [1 mark for rounding at least one number to 1 s.f.]
5. $500 \div 34$ [1] $= 14.7$g [1]
6. $70 \times 40 \times 60$ [1] $= 168\,000$ [1]
   £1680 [1]
7. 1.65m [1] $\leqslant x < 1.75$m [1]

   0.05 above and below 1.7

Module 7: Answers Using Technology

1. **(a)** 410.0625 **(b)** 7 **(c)** 5

2. **(a)** $\dfrac{19.21}{32.76}$ [1] $= 0.586\,385\,836$ [1]

   (b) $\sqrt{28.8}$ [1] $= 5.366\,563\,146$ [1]

   Do not round at any point.

3. **(a)** 1.715×10^8 **(b)** 1.2×10^5

4. **(a)** $2\dfrac{20}{21}$

   Your calculator might show `2⌐20⌐21`

(b) $31\frac{1}{18}$

5. (a) $1.496 \times 10^8 \div 400$ **[1]** $= 374\,000$ **[1]** $= 3.74 \times 10^5$ km **[1]**
   (b) $1.392 \times 10^6 \div 3.48 \times 10^3$ **[1]** $= 400$ **[1]** $= 4 \times 10^2$ **[1]**

Module 8: Algebraic Notation

1. (a) $5a + 2$ **(b)** $15h + 2k$ **(c)** $-2a + 2b$ **(d)** $8x^2 - x + 1$

2. (a) $6p^7$ **(b)** $27p^{12}$ **(c)** $6f^5g$ **(d)** $\dfrac{1}{8p^6}$

3. (a) $12k^2$ **(b)** a^3 **(c)** $p^{\frac{5}{2}}$

   (d) $p^{\frac{13}{2}}$ or $\sqrt{p^{13}}$

4. (a) $\dfrac{1}{4}$ **(b)** $\dfrac{25}{4}$

   (c) 4 **(d)** 1

5. (a) Equation **(b)** Identity **(c)** Identity

   (d) Equation **(e)** Equation

Module 9: Algebraic Expressions

1. (a) $6a - 12$ **[2]**
   (b) $3m^2 + 6m$ **[2]**
   (c) $8n^2 - 4np$ **[2]**
   (d) $8d + 2$ **[2]**
   (e) $4x + 22$ **[2]**

> Remember in the last bracket, $-2 \times -3 = +6$

2. (a) $a^2 + 3a + 2a + 6$ **[1]** $= a^2 + 5a + 6$ **[1]**
   (b) $f^2 + 6f - 5f - 30$ **[1]** $= f^2 + f - 30$ **[1]**
   (c) $x^2 - 5x - 7x + 35$ **[1]** $= x^2 - 12x + 35$ **[1]**
   (d) $a^2 + 4a + 4a + 16$ **[1]** $= a^2 + 8a + 16$ **[1]**

> Remember $(a + 4)^2$ means $(a + 4)(a + 4)$, **not** $a^2 + 16$

   (e) $a^2 - 9a - 9a + 81$ **[1]** $= a^2 - 18a + 81$ **[1]**

3. (a) $3(a - b)$ **[2]**
   (b) $2(3p + 4)$ **[2]**
   (c) $x(x - 7)$ **[2]**
   (d) $2q(p - 3)$ **[2]**
   (e) $5p(p - 2)$ **[2]**

4. $6x - 3 + 4x + 32 + 5$ **[1]** $= 10x + 34$ **[1]** $= 2(5x + 17)$ **[1]**

5. (a) $(p + 3)(p + 1)$ **[2]**
   (b) $(x - 3)(x - 7)$ **[2]**
   (c) $(a + 11)(a + 1)$ **[2]**
   (d) $(x + 3)(x - 4)$ **[2]**

6. (a) $(t + 3)(t - 3)$ **[2]**
   (b) $(4 + f)(4 - f)$ **[2]**
   (c) $(1 + 5n)(1 - 5n)$ **[2]**
   (d) $(t + 5)(t - 5)$ **[2]**
   (e) $(p^4 + 2)(p^4 - 2)$ **[2]**

Module 10: Algebraic Formulae

1. (a) 36 **(b)** -8 **(c)** 8

   (d) -5 **(e)** 6

2. $v - u = at$ **[1]**
   $a = \dfrac{v - u}{t}$ **[1]**

3. $5y = 2 + x$ **[1]**
   $x = 5y - 2$ **[1]**

4. $xy - 8y = 2 + 3x$ **[1]**

   $xy - 3x = 2 + 8y$
   $x(y - 3) = 2 + 8y$ **[1]**
   $x = \dfrac{2 + 8y}{y - 3}$ **[1]**

5. $q = r - p$ **[2]**

> Try to write the given information mathematically first. This question is basically telling you that $p + q = r$, then asking you to rearrange the equation.

6. (a) 31.1 degrees Celsius (1 d.p.)
   (b) $9T_C = 5T_F - 160$ **[1]**

   $T_F = \dfrac{9T_C}{5} + 32$ **[1]**

   (c) 140 degrees Fahrenheit

Module 11: Algebraic Equations

1. $4x = 36$ **[1]**
   $x = 9$ **[1]**

2. $5x - 10 - 3x + 12 = 4$ **[1]**
   $2x = 2$
   $x = 1$ **[1]**

3. $3(x + 4) = 5(x - 2)$ **[1]**

> You can 'cross multiply' by 3 and 5 to clear the fraction here.

   $3x + 12 = 5x - 10$ **[1]**
   $2x = 22$
   $x = 11$ **[1]**

4. $(x + 9)(x + 4) = 0$ **[1]**
   $x = -9$ or $x = -4$ **[2]**

5. $(x - 7)(x + 4) = 0$ **[1]**
   $x = 7$ or $x = -4$ **[2]**

6. $(4x - 3y = 14$ and$)$ $3x + 3y = 21$ **[1]**
   $7x = 35$ **[1]**
   $x = 5$ **[1]**
   $y = 2$ **[1]**

7. $8x + 4y = 20$ (and $3x + 4y = 10$) **[1]**
   $5x = 10$ **[1]**
   $x = 2$ **[1]**
   $y = 1$ **[1]**

8. (a) $x = 0.7$, $x = 6.3$ **[2]**
   (b) $x = -0.5$, $x = 7.5$ **[2]**

> Remember to start with the equation you are trying to solve, i.e. $x^2 - 7x - 4 = 0$. You then get to $x^2 - 7x + 4$ by adding 8 to both sides of the equation. So draw the line $y = 8$ and see where the curve crosses.

Module 12: Algebraic Inequalities

1. $7x > 35$ **[1]**
   $x > 5$ **[1]**

2. $-3x \geqslant 3$ **[1]**
   $x \leqslant -1$ **[1]**

3. $38 > -2x$ **[1]**
   $-19 < x$ **[1]**
   $x > -19$ **[1]**

4. (a) $x \leqslant -1$ **(b)** $x > 3$ **(c)** $-4 \leqslant x < 2$

5. $x = -1, 0, 1, 2, 3, 4$ **[2]**

6. $x = -7, -6, -5, -4$ **[2]**

7. $x = 2, 3, 4, 5, 6$ **[2]**

8. $5 < 10x$ **[1]**
   $\dfrac{1}{2} < x$ $x > \dfrac{1}{2}$ **[1]**

> Always rewrite your answer so it starts with '$x...$'

   -5 -4 -3 -2 -1 0 1 2 3 4 5 **[1]**

9. $2x - 3 > 5$
   $2x > 8$ **[1]**
   $x > 4$ **[1]**
   AND
   $12 - x > 6$

$-x > -6$ **[1]**

$x < 6$ **[1]**

So $x = 5$ **[1]**

10. $x = 4, 5, 6, 7, 8, 9, 10, 11$ **[2]**

Module 13: Sequences

1. 24, 28 **[1 for each correct term]**

2. 5, -4 **[1 for each correct term]**

3. 1, 3, 13, 63, 313 **[2 if fully correct; 1 if one error]**

4. 8, 17, 26, 35 **[2 if fully correct; 1 if one error]**

5. **(a)** $U_n = 4n + 7$ **[1 for 4n; 1 for 7]**

(b) Yes **[1]** since there is a whole number solution to $4n + 7 = 303$
($n = 74$) **[1]**

6. **(a)** $a = 15$, $d = 2$ **[2]**

(b) $U_n = 2n + 13$ **[2]**

7. $\dfrac{1}{3}, \dfrac{1}{9}, \dfrac{1}{27}, \dfrac{1}{81}$ **[4]**

Module 14: Coordinates and Linear Functions

1. Line A: 6 **[1]**   Line B: -3 **[1]**   Line C: $\dfrac{-2}{3}$ **[1]**   Line D: 1 **[1]**

2. Lines A and C are parallel. **[2]**

Rearrange each equation to make y the subject. You can then see clearly what the gradient is.

3. $x = 0$

4. $y = -6x + 9$ **[2]**

You are told m and c in the question, so you can write the answer straight down by substituting these values into $y = mx + c$

5. $y = 5x + c$ **[1]**

$1 = -15 + c$ **[1]**

$c = 16$ **[1]**

$y = 5x + 16$

6.

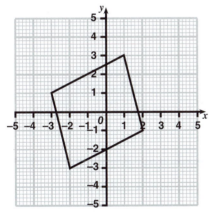

First three vertices plotted correctly **[1]**
Fourth vertex at $(-2, -3)$ **[2]**

7. $m = \dfrac{-5 - (-10)}{6 - (-4)}$ **[1]**

$m = \dfrac{1}{2}$

$y = \dfrac{1}{2}x + c$ **[1]**

Substitute in one coordinate to give $c = -8$ **[1]**

$y = \dfrac{1}{2}x - 8$ **[1]**

Always show your working out for the gradient. Even if the final answer is wrong, you will still pick up some marks.

Module 15: Quadratic Functions

1. **(a)** $x = -5$, $x = 3$ **[2]**

The roots will be where the curve crosses the x-axis.

(b) $(0, -15)$ **[1]**

(c) $(-1, -16)$ **[2]**

2. $(x + 4)(x - 11) = 0$ **[1]**

$x + 4 = 0$ or $x - 11 = 0$

$x = -4$ **[1]** or $x = 11$ **[1]**

3. **(a)** $x = -1.4$, $x = 3.4$ (or $x = -1.5$, $x = 3.5$) **[2]**

(b) $(0, 5)$ **[1]**

(c) $x = 1$ **[2]**

4. **(a)** $x = 4$ **[2]**

Use $x = \dfrac{-b}{2a}$ for the line of symmetry when you don't have the curve.

(b) $(4, -13)$ **[2]**

Module 16: Other Functions

1. 0 $\rightarrow$ 5 **[1]**

   1       $\rightarrow$ 17 **[1]**

   2       $\rightarrow$ 29 **[1]**

2. $f(x) = 3x - 3$ **[2]**

3. $x = 5, 6, 7$ **[3]**

To find the first 'input' you just solve the equation $\dfrac{x + 3}{2} = 4$

4. **(a)** **(i)** General shape **[1]** going through origin. **[1]**

   (ii) Two parts **[1]** both not crossing axes. **[1]**

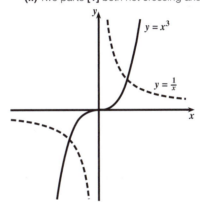

When sketching two graphs on the same axes, make sure they cross in (approximately) the right place.

(b) 2

5. Line 1: $y = x^2 - x^3$ **[1]**
Line 2: $y = x$ **[1]**
Line 3: $y = x^2 - x$ **[1]**
Line 4: $y = -\dfrac{2}{x}$ **[1]**

6.

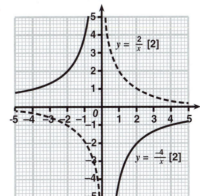

$y = \dfrac{2}{x}$ **[2]**

$y = -\dfrac{4}{x}$ **[2]**

Module 17: Problems and Graphs

1. **(a)** 11.30am

(b) $1\dfrac{1}{2}$ hours

(c) $\frac{6}{1.5}$ **[1]** = 4km/h **[1]**

2. **(a)** $\frac{30}{10}$ **[1]** = 3m/s² **[1]**

   (b) 5 + 10 = 15s

   (c) $\left(\frac{1}{2} \times 10 \times 30\right)$ + (5 × 30) **[1]** = 150 + 150 = 300m **[1]**

3. **(a)** £3

   > The standing charge is the cost of getting into the taxi before actually travelling any distance.

   (b) £7.50

   (c) $\frac{6}{8}$ **[1]**

   $= \frac{3}{4}$ of £1

   = 75p **[1]**

   > The cost per mile is the gradient. As this is a straight line, it will not matter which two points you choose to calculate the gradient.

Module 18: Converting Measurements

1. 0.85 × 1.25 (or 850 × 1250) **[1]**
   = 1.06m² (3 s.f.) (or 1 062 500mm²) **[1]**
2. 3.4 × 1000² **[1]** = 3 400 000m² **[1]**
3. 100 × 100 × 100cm³ = 1m³ **[1]**
   1 000 000g = 1000kg **[1]**
4. 68 ÷ 5 × 8 or 110 ÷ 8 × 5 **[1]**
   108.8 or 68.75
   110km/h is faster **[1]**
5. 24 × 60 × 60m/hour **[1]** ÷ 1000 **[1]** = 86.4km/h **[1]**

   > Multiply m/s by 60 × 60 to convert to m/hr.

6. **(a)** Bob 626 ÷ 35 = £17.89/h **[1]**
      Leila 30 000 ÷ (32 × 52) **[1]** = £18.03/h
      Shahida has best hourly rate. **[1]**
   (b) Shahida 18.4 × 30 × 52 = £28 704
      Bob 626 × 52 = £32 552
      [1 for either Bob or Shahida correct]
      Bob earns most per year. **[1]**

      > 1 year = 52 weeks

7. **(a)** 463 ÷ 24 **[1]** = 19.29g/cm³ (2 d.p.) **[1]**
   (b) 19.29… × 30 **[1]** = 578.75g **[1]**
   (c) (463 + 578.75) × 23.50 **[1]** = £24 481.13 **[1]**
      [No mark for 24 481.125]

Module 19: Scales, Diagrams and Maps

1. **(a)** 3 × 20 = 60m
   (b) 57 ÷ 20 **[1]** = 2.85m **[1]**

   > Scale 1 : *n* means 1 and *n* given in cm. Convert *n* to m or km as necessary.

2. **(a)** 5.3cm to 5.5cm
   (b) 5.3 × 5 000 000 **[1]** = 265km **[1]** **[Accept up to 275km for a 5.5cm measurement]**
   (c) 203° (±3°) **[2]**
      [1 mark for correct construction or 157°]
   (d) (203) − 180 OR (203) + 180 − 360 **[1]** = 023° **[1]**

3. **(a)**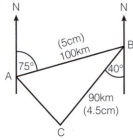

   [1 for correct drawing; 1 for accuracy]

(b) 318° (±3°) **[1]**
   58km (±2km) **[1]**

> All bearings are measured clockwise from the North line.

4. **(a)** 18 × 25 000 **[1]** = 450 000cm = 4.5km **[1]**
   (b) **[2]**

   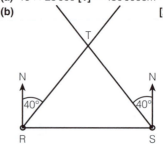

   [1 for one bearing correct]

Module 20: Comparing Quantities

1. 37.5% $\frac{14}{5}$ $3\frac{5}{8}$

   [2 if fully correct; 1 for two correct]

2. 20%   0.21   0.211 $\frac{2}{9}$ $\frac{3}{10}$

   [2 if fully correct; 1 for four in correct order]

   > Change all amounts to decimals to find the correct order.

3. 2.8 − 2.5 = 0.3
   2.5 − 2.125 = 0.375 **[1]**
   0.3 < 0.375 so $2\frac{4}{5}$ closer **[1] [or equivalent working in fractions]**

4. $\frac{3}{8} \times \frac{5}{6}$ **[1]** $= \frac{5}{16}$ = 31.25% **[1]**

   OR $\frac{5}{6}$ of 12 = 10 **[1]**

   $\frac{10}{32}$ = 31.25% **[1]**

5. **(a)** 2.54 ÷ 3.45 OR 5.99 ÷ 3.45 **[1]** → 73.6% (1 d.p.) **[1]**
   (b) 3.45 × 1.15 **[1]** (= £3.97)
      (3.45 × 1.15) × 80 **[1]** (= £317.40)
      55 × 6.99 + 25 × 4 **[1]** = £484.45
      £484.45 − £317.40 = £167.05
      167.05 ÷ 317.40 = 52.6% **[1]**

      > Percentage profit = (profit ÷ original amount) × 100

6. **(a)** 0.4 × 0.55 **[1]** + 0.65 × (1 − 0.55) **[1]** = 51.25% **[1]**
   (b) $\frac{35}{100}$ **[1]** $= \frac{7}{20}$ **[1]**

Module 21: Ratio

1. 20cm : 3m **[1]** simplifies to 2 : 30 **[1]** All the rest simplify to 2 : 3

   > Divide all parts of the ratio by a common factor.

2. **(a)** 1 + 2 + 7 **[1]** = 10
      2 litres ÷ 10 **[1]** = 200ml
      Navy blue: 200ml; Grey: 400ml; White: 1400ml **[1]**
   (b) 1200 ÷ 2 = 600ml and 6000 ÷ 7 = 857ml so grey is limiting colour **[1]**
      1 lot is 600ml so total 600 × 10 = 6000ml = 6 litres **[1]**

3. A is $\frac{5}{8}$ of B

4. **(a)** 50 ÷ 5 = 10 so 3 biscuits need 10g.
      3 × 7 = 21 biscuits
      [1 for any correct method; 1 for correct answer]
   (b) 175 ÷ 5 = 35 so 35g flour for 3 biscuits.
      35 × 4 = 140g
      [1 for any correct method; 1 for correct answer]

5. No
   Blue costs 30 ÷ 5 **[1]** = £6/litre and yellow 28 ÷ 7 = £4/litre
   Cost for 7 litres 5 × 4 + 2 × 6 **[1]** = £32
   Lucy gets £4.50 × 7 = £31.50. So she loses 50p **[1]**

Module 22: Proportion

1. 59×2.5 **[1]** $= 147.5$kcal **[1]**
2. (a) $500 \times 1.29 = €645$
   (b) $(645 - 570) \div 1.33$ **[1]** $= £56.39$ **[1]**

   > Each £ receives €1.29 → multiply. Each €1.33 receives £1 → divide.

3. (a) $1360 \div 80$ **[1]** $= 17$ litres/cow
   $17 \times (80 + 25)$ **[1]** $= 1785$
   $1785 \times 365 \times 0.3$ **[1]** $= £195\,457.50$ **[1]**
   (b) $800 \div 105 = 7.6$ days
   [1 for any correct method; 1 for correct answer]

   > 6 tonnes is 800 cattle feeds.

4. Scale factor $\times 1.5$ **[1]**
   $PR = 6 \div 1.5$ **[1]** $= 4$cm
   $TU = 4.5 \times 1.5 = 6.75$cm
   [1 for both correct values]

   > Scale factor $= \dfrac{9}{6} = 1.5$

5. (a) $\dfrac{270}{120}$ **[1]** $= \dfrac{9}{4}$
   (b) Scale factor for length $= \sqrt{\dfrac{9}{4}}$ **[1]** $= \dfrac{3}{2}$ **[1]**
   (c) Scale factor for volume $= \dfrac{27}{8}$ **[1]**
   Volume of P $= 2700 \div \dfrac{27}{8}$ **[1]** $= 800$cm³ **[1]**

Module 23: Rates of Change

1. (a) $10\,000 \times 1.02^4$ or other stepwise method **[1]**
   $= £10\,824.32$ **[1]**
   [1 for $10\,000 \times 1.02$]
   (b) $10\,000 \times 1.15$ **[1]** $\times 1.06 \times 0.82 \times 1.01$ **[1]**
   $= £10\,095.76$ **[1]**

2. No **[1]**
   $6500 \times 1.03 = 6695$ so £195 is correct for first year but the money invested for year 2 is $6500 + 195$ so it will earn more interest **[1]**.
   Actual interest $= 6500 \times 1.03^3 - 6500 = £602.73$ **[1]**

3. (a) 20cm   (b) Between 4 and 8 minutes   (c) $20 \div 4 = 5$cm/min

   > Steepest gradient gives fastest speed.

4. (a) Line drawn from $t = 8$ to the curve **[1]**
   96m **[1]**
   (b) $210 \div 10$ **[1]** $= 21$m/s (± 0.4m/s) **[1]**

Module 24: Constructions

1. **[1 for correct construction lines shown; 1 for accuracy]**

   > Always leave your construction lines and arcs, the examiner needs to see them.

2. **[1 for width 3.5cm; 1 for accurate lengths and 90° angles]**
3. **[1 for correct construction; 1 (conditional on construction) for angle of 90° (±2°)]**
4.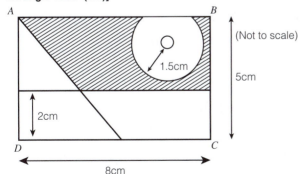

   [1 for circle radius 1.5cm around tree; 1 for line 2cm from DC; 1 for correct area shaded]
5. **[1 for equilateral triangle used to construct 60°; 1 for construction of angle bisector; 1 (conditional on construction) for angle of 30° (±2°)]**

Module 25: Angles

1. For tessellation, the angles must sum to 360°.
   Internal angle of a regular pentagon $= 108°$
   $360 \div 108$ is not a whole number.
   [1 for 108°; 1 for written or diagrammatic explanation]

2. $180 - 135$ **[1]** $= 45$
   $360 \div 45 = 8$ **[1]**

   > It is always the **external** angles that sum to 360°.

3. Internal angle of hexagon $= 120°$
   Internal angle of octagon $= 135°$
   [1 for one correct method]
   $360 - (120 + 135)$ **[1]** $= 105°$ **[1]**

4. Triangle ABC <u>isosceles</u>
   Angle $ACB =$ <u>$180 - 2 \times 70$</u> **[1]** $= 40°$
   Angle $FCD = 40°$ (<u>vertically opposite angles are equal</u>)
   Angle $FED = 360 - (130 + 130 + 40) = 60°$ **[1]**
   (<u>angles in a quadrilateral sum to 360°</u>)
   [1 for all four underlined reasons]

   > Give a reason for each step of your working.

5. e.g. $\angle BPQ = 65°$ (vertically opposite angles equal)
   $\angle PRQ = 180 - 120 = 60°$ (angles on straight line sum to 180°)
   $\angle CPR = 60°$ **[1]** (alternate angles are equal)
   [1 for any correct, complete reasons]

Module 26: Properties of 2D Shapes

1. A – equilateral, B – obtuse isosceles, C – obtuse scalene, D – right-angled isosceles, E – scalene
   [3 if fully correct; 2 if three correct; 1 if one correct]
2. $\angle QBC = c$ (alternate angles are equal) **[1]**
   $\angle PBA = a$ (alternate angles are equal) **[1]**
   $a + b + c = 180°$ (angle sum on straight line $= 180°$) **[1]**
   Therefore angles in a triangle sum to 180°.

   > A proof must work for every possible value so you will need to use algebra.

3. All angles at centre are equal and $360 \div 8 = 45°$
   All triangles isosceles so base angle $= (180 - 45) \div 2$ **[1]** $= 67.5°$
   1 internal angle $= 2 \times 67.5$ **[1]** $= 135°$
   Total $= 135 \times 8 = 1080°$ **[1]**
4. kite
5. Internal angle of an octagon $= 135°$
   Internal angle of an equilateral triangle $= 60°$ **[1 for either 135 or 60]**
   Angles at a point $= 360°$ so $x = 360 - (135 + 90 + 60)$ **[1]** $= 75°$
   [1]

Module 27: Congruence and Similarity

1. B and E

   > Similar means all angles the same / pairs of sides in the same ratio.

2. G and I

   > Congruent = same shape **and** size

3. (a) $\dfrac{12}{8}$ or $\dfrac{8}{12}$ or 1.5 **[1]**
   $6 \times 1.5 = 9$cm **[1]**
   (b) $10 \div 1.5$ **[1]** $= \dfrac{20}{3}$ or $6\dfrac{2}{3}$ or 6.67cm **[1]**
4. Yes, both right angled with sides 3, 4, 5cm **[1]**, so SSS (or RHS) **[1]**
5. No. **[1]**
   A comparison of ratio **[1]**
   $\dfrac{156}{85} = 1.835 \neq \dfrac{142}{75} = 1.893$ or $\dfrac{156}{142} = 1.096 \neq \dfrac{85}{75} = 1.133$ (3 d.p.) **[1]**

Module 28: Transformations

1. (a) Reflection **[1]** in $y = x + 1$ **[1]**
   (b) Reflection in $x = -1$ **[2 if fully correct; 1 if line drawn only]**

2. Enlargement **[1]**, scale factor $\frac{1}{2}$ **[1]**, centre (0, 0) **[1]**

   Write one fact for each mark.

3.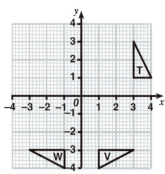

   (a) Correct plot
   (b) **[2 if fully correct; 1 for rotation]**

   Make sure you do the transformation on the correct shape.

   (c) **[2 if fully correct; 1 for reflection of V if it was incorrect in part (b)]**
   (d) Rotation, centre (0,0) **[1]**,
   90° anti-clockwise **or**
   270° clockwise **[1]**

4.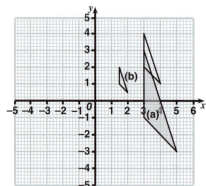

   (a) **[2 if fully correct; 1 for correct scale factor × 2]**
   (b) **[2 if fully correct; 1 for correct scale factor × 0.5]**

Module 29: Circles

1. (a) radius   (b) diameter
   (c) tangent   (d) circumference
   (e) arc   (f) sector
   (g) segment   (h) isosceles

2. $\pi \times 9$ **[1]** = 28.274… **[1]**

   = 28cm **[1]**

   Make sure you know (and use) the correct formula.

3. $\pi \times 4^2$ **[1]** = 16π **[1]** cm² **[1]**

   Here the diameter is given but you need the radius to work out area.

4. $\frac{\pi \times 5}{2} + 8 + \frac{\pi \times 5}{2} + 8$ (or equivalent) **[1]** = $5\pi + 16$
   = 31.7cm **[1]**

5. $\pi \times 10^2 \div 4$ **[1]** + $\pi \times 2.5^2$ = 98.174 777 **[1]** cm² **[1]**
   = 98.2cm² **[1]**

6. Radius of plane's journey is 6381 **[1]**

   $\pi \times 2 \times 6381 - \pi \times 2 \times 6370$ **[1]**

   or $2 \times \pi \times 11$ **[1]** = 69.1km **[1]**

Module 30: Properties of 3D Shapes

1. Pentagonal-based **[1]** pyramid **[1]**
2. A square-based pyramid **[1]** and triangular prism **[1]** accurately represented by diagrams **[1]**

3.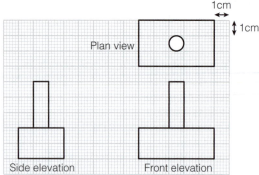

   [1 for each drawing; 1 for accuracy]

4.  **[3]**

Module 31: Perimeter, Area and Volume

1. (a) Area: 8×3 **[1]** = 24m² **[1]**
   Perimeter: 26m **[1]**
   (b) Area: $\frac{1}{2} \times 14 \times 3$ **[1]** = 21cm² **[1]**
   Perimeter: 22.6cm **[1]**

2. $200 \times 80 - 25 \times 20$ **[1]** = 15 500cm² **[1]** (or equivalent calculation to 1.55m²)

3. (a) $\frac{100 \times 80}{2}$ or $\frac{1 \times 0.8}{2}$ **[1]** = 4000cm² or 0.4m² **[1]**

   (b) $\frac{1}{2}(60 + 80) \times (100 - 75)$ or other correct method **[1]** = 1750cm² **[1]**

   (c) $\frac{75 \times 60}{2} - \pi \times 12.5^2$ **[1]** = 1759.126… cm² **[1]** = 1760cm² (3 s.f.)

4. $(\pi \times 4^2 \times 2)$ **[1]** + $(\pi \times 8 \times 5)$ **[1]** = $32\pi + 40\pi = 72\pi$cm² **[1]**

5. $3^3 + \frac{1}{3}\pi \times 1.5^2 \times 4$ **[1]** = 36.4 **[1]** cm³ **[1]**

6. $\frac{4}{3}\pi \times 3.5^3 = a^3$ **[1]**
   $a^3 = 179.59$ **[1]**
   $a = 5.64$cm (3 s.f.) **[1]**

7. $\frac{2}{3}\pi \times 5^3$ **[1]** = $\frac{250}{3}\pi$ **[1]** cm³ **[1]**

8. Surface area of cuboid $2 \times (4.4 \times 5.3 + 4.4 \times 1.8 + 5.3 \times 1.8)$ **[1]**
   = 81.6cm²
   Surface area of hemisphere $2\pi r^2 + \pi r^2$ **[1]** = $3 \times \pi \times 2.8^2$ **[1]**
   = 73.9cm²

   Cuboid larger **[1 from correct values]**

Module 32: Pythagoras' Theorem and Trigonometry

1. (a) $\cos p = \frac{2.8}{3.5}$ **[1]** = 0.8 **[1]**

   $p = 36.9°$ **[1]**

   (b) $\tan 51° = \frac{KL}{10.5}$ **[1]**

   $KL = 12.966$ **[1]** = 13.0m **[1]**

2. (a) $6^2 + NP^2 = 7^2$ **[1]**

   $NP = \sqrt{7^2 - 6^2} = 3.61$cm (3 s.f.) **[1]**

   (b) $\tan NOP = \frac{NP}{5.5}$ **[1]** = 0.6555

   Angle $NOP = \tan^{-1}0.6555$ **[1]** = 33.2° (3 s.f.) **[1]**

3. $9^2 = 7^2 + q^2$ **[1]**

   Substitute the values in the Pythagoras equation and then rearrange it.

   $q^2 = 9^2 - 7^2$ **[1]** = 32
   $q = \sqrt{32}$ (or $4\sqrt{2}$) **[1]**

4. (a) (i) $\frac{1}{\sqrt{2}}$ or $\frac{\sqrt{2}}{2}$ (ii) 1

(b) $a = 2 \times \sin 60° = 2 \times \dfrac{\sqrt{3}}{2}$ **[1]** $= \sqrt{3}$ cm **[1]**

$b = 2 \times \cos 60° = 2 \times \dfrac{1}{2}$ **[1]** $= 1$cm **[1]**

5. $\sin x = \dfrac{1}{5}$ **[1]**

$x = \sin^{-1}\dfrac{1}{5}$ **[1]** $= 11.5°$ **[1]**

Module 33: Vectors

1. **a = 2r**   **b = −3s**

   c = r + t   **d = 2t − s** or **d = r + t − 2s**

   [1 for each correct answer]

2. **(a)** **b**   **(b)** −**b**

   (c) **a + c**   **(d)** **a − b**

   (e) **b − a − c** (or equivalent)

   (f) **c + a − $\dfrac{1}{2}$ b** (or equivalent)

3. **(a)** $\overrightarrow{BE} = -2\mathbf{b}$

   (b) $\overrightarrow{AC} = \mathbf{b} + \mathbf{d}$ **[2]**

   (c) $\overrightarrow{CE} = \overrightarrow{CB} + \overrightarrow{BE} = -2\mathbf{b} - \mathbf{d}$ **[2]**

   > The opposite sides of a parallelogram are described with equal vectors.

4. $\overrightarrow{OR} = 2\mathbf{q}$ **[1]**

   $\overrightarrow{PQ} = \mathbf{q} - \mathbf{p}$ **[1]**

   $\overrightarrow{PR} = 2\mathbf{q} - \mathbf{p}$ **[1]**

Module 34: Experimental and Theoretical Probability

1.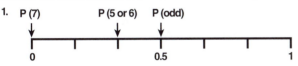

2. **(a)** $\dfrac{4}{14}$ or $\dfrac{2}{7}$ **(b)** $\dfrac{5}{14}$ **(c)** $\dfrac{9}{14}$

3. $1 - (0.2 + 0.3 + 0.25 + 0.1)$ **[1]** $= 0.15$ **[1]**

4. **(a)** $\dfrac{12}{25}$ or 0.48

   (b) $3 + 4 + 12 = 19$ **[1]**

   $\dfrac{19}{25} \times 250$ **[1]** $= 190$ **[1]**

Module 35: Representing Probability

1. (1, head), (1, tail), (2, head), (2, tail), (3, head), (3, tail), (4, head), (4, tail), (5, head), (5, tail), (6, head), (6, tail)

   [2 for all 12 outcomes; 1 if one missing or repeated answers have been included]

2. **(a)**

	Dice					
	1	**2**	**3**	**4**	**5**	**6**
1	2	3	4	5	6	7
3	4	5	6	7	8	9
5	6	7	8	9	10	11

   (Spinner on the left axis)

   [2 if fully correct; 1 for two correct rows or four correct columns]

   (b) $\dfrac{6}{18}$ or $\dfrac{1}{3}$ **(c)** $\dfrac{9}{18}$ or $\dfrac{1}{2}$

   > Only count the 18 outcomes, not the numbers on the dice and spinner.

3. **(a)**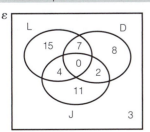

[3 if fully correct; 2 for six correct numbers; 1 for three correct numbers]

> 0 in the middle since no one can vote for all three. All the numbers in the diagram must add up to 50.

(b) $\dfrac{11}{50}$

Module 36: Data and Averages

1. **(a)** 498   **(b)** 499

   > The median is between 498 and 500 and so is 499.

   (c) Any suitable answers, e.g. The sample size is too small. Need to sample across the range of times during production.

   [1 for each reason up to a maximum of 2]

2. **(a)** $60 \leqslant w < 80$

   > Median value is between the 80th and 81st value, which is in the $60 \leqslant w < 80$ class interval.

   (b) Correct midpoints (35, 45, 55, 70, 90, 110, 135) **[1]**
   Correct total of midpoint × frequency of 10 915 **[1]**
   Estimated mean = 68.2g **[1]**

   (c) $20 + 25 + 22 + 44 = 111$ **[1]**
   $111 \div 160 = 69.4\%$ **[1]**

3. 6, 6, 6, 7, 10 or 6, 6, 6, 8, 9 **[3]** Other solutions are possible.

   [1 mark for any one of and 2 marks for any two of: a total of 35, median of 6 or mode of 6]

   > The total of all five numbers must be 35, i.e. 5 (cards) × 7 (mean) = 35

Module 37: Statistical Diagrams

1. **(a)** 21

   (b) A bar chart or vertical line graph, with frequency on the y-axis and days of the week on the x-axis, e.g.

   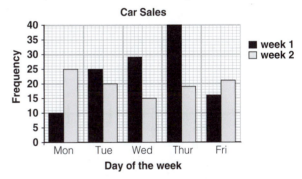

   [1 for selecting a dual bar chart or vertical line diagram; 1 for fully correct data (frequencies for each bars); 1 for a fully labelled chart]

2. Biscuit Treats: 21 **[1]**
   Meaty Sticks: 5 **[1]**
   Sum to 60 **[1]**

   > Place the known data into the Venn diagram starting with the overlap (buy both).

   (Venn diagram: ε with Biscuit Treats 21, overlap 14, Meaty Sticks 5, and 20 outside)

3. Table completed as follows:
   Seafood – 106.7°; Meat – 66.7°;
   Chicken – 53.3°; Mushroom – 55 and 73.3° **[1 for correct frequency of mushroom and 1 for correct angles]**

   > Total frequency must be 45 × 6 = 270 as vegetarian represents one-sixth of the pie chart. 270 − 215 = 55 mushroom

4. **(a)** Attempt to draw a graph to interpret the data **[1]**
   Appropriate line of best fit drawn **[1]**
   Estimate 175–195 million **[1]**

   (b) Any suitable answer, e.g. It would not be reliable to use the graph to predict sales in year 14 because it is beyond the range of the data **[1]** and the trend of sales may change **[1]**.

5. **(a)** A scatter graph drawn with age on x-axis and speed on y-axis **[1]** and the points correctly plotted **[1]**. Data supports John's conclusion. **[1]**

(b) Negative correlation

The trend shows that the younger the driver, the higher the speed; and the older the driver, the lower the speed. So the correlation is negative.

Module 38: Comparing Distributions

1.

	Represents a single value	Affected by outliers	Measure of spread
Mode	✓	✗	✗
Median	✓	✗	✗
Mean	✗	✓	✗
Range	✗	✓	✓

[2 if fully correct; 1 if one error]

2. Class A: Median 45, Mean 48.8 **[2]**
   Class B: Median 42, Mean 45.7 **[2]**
   Any suitable conclusion, e.g. Class A has a higher mean and a higher median; or Class B is more consistent **[1]**

   Find the mean and median for the two groups of data and then compare.

3. **(a)** Mean will be higher as her distance is higher than current mean.
   (b) The median may be higher as it's also higher than current median but you can't be certain without knowing the other values.
4. Calculation of estimated mean: £244 for 30–50 year olds and £329 for under 30s **[2]**
   Median intervals of $200 \leq c < 250$ for 30–50 year olds and $300 \leq c < 350$ for under 30s **[1]**
   [1 mark for a suitable comparison of the estimated means]
   [1 mark for a suitable comparison of median intervals]

Practice Exam Paper 1

1. **(a)** 26
   (b) 0.3
   (c) $\frac{15}{100}$ **[1]** $= \frac{3}{20}$ **[1]**
2. Mean
3.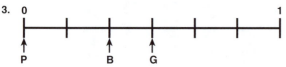

   [2 for three correct; 1 for two correct]
4. $-5 - 3 = -8$ **[1]**
   $-8 \div 4 = -2$ **[1]**

   Work backwards

5. **(a)** Any suitable reasons, e.g. higher mean or median
   (b) Performance more consistent (range 88 vs 132)
6. 1, 2, 4, 5, 8, 10, 20, 40

   [2 if fully correct; 1 for 5–7 correct factors]
7. **(a)** 27
   (b) 10 000
   (c) 2
8. $\frac{12}{20} + \frac{5}{20}$ **[1]** $= \frac{17}{20}$ **[1]**

   Find equivalent fractions with a common denominator.

9. Ann got two lots more than Timmy.

   1 lot $\frac{£32}{2}$ = £16 **[1 for showing correct division]**
   George got (16) × 5 **[1 for your answer × 5]** = £80 **[1]**

   Read the question carefully.

10. **(a)** $\left(\frac{20 \times 9}{4}\right) \times 3$ **[1]** = £135 **[1]**

    Round each number to 1 significant figure.

11. **(b)** 885 × 22 = 19 470 **[1]**
    8.85 × 22 = £194.70 **[1]**

    Use long multiplication and count decimal places or use your own method.

11. Attempts to add both equations **[1]**
    $6x = 6$ **[1]**
    $x = 1$ **[1]**
    $y = -3$ **[1]**
12. P(orange) = $\frac{2}{3}$ **[1]**

    $\frac{2}{3}$ of 9 = 6 **[1]**

    To start with there was a multiple of 3 chocolates and then a multiple of 4 after 1 had been eaten. So there must have been 9 chocolates to start with.

13. 10% = 34, so 5% = 17 **[1]**
    340 + 34 + 17 = £391 **[1 for correct answer including units]**

14.

		Second roll			
		Blue	Green	White	Red
First roll	Blue	B, B	B, G	B, W	B, R
	Green	G, B	G, G	G, W	G, R
	White	W, B	W, G	W, W	W, R
	Red	R, B	R, G	R, W	R, R

[2 if fully correct; 1 for at least two columns or two rows correct]

15. $a = -1$ and $b = 7$, $a = -4$ and $b = 4$, $a = -11$ and $b = 2$,
    $a = -25$ and $b = 1$
    [1 mark for each correct pair of answers]

    Since a must be a negative number, the solution $a = 1$, $b = 14$ is invalid.

16. $\frac{15}{16}$

    Turn the second fraction upside down and multiply.

17. **(a)** $\frac{4}{6}$ **[1]** $= \frac{2}{3}$
    (b) $BC^2 + 4^2 = 6^2$ **[1 for correct use of Pythagoras]**
    $BC = \sqrt{6^2 - 4^2}$ **[1]** $= \sqrt{20}$ **[1]**
18. $x = -1$ **[1]**
    $x = 9$ **[1]**
19. **(a)** 1400 ÷ (14 + 15 + 21) **[1]** = 28
    28 × 15 = £420 **[1]**
    (b) Less.
    1400 ÷ (16 + 17 + 23) **[1]** = 25
    (£25 × 23) = £575 **[1]** and (£28 × 21) = £588 **[1]**
20. $9x^4 y^{10}$ **[2]**
21. Using the bar chart to find correct total of years
    1, 2, 3, 5 = 95 **[1]**
    TV sales: 120 − 95 = 25 (i.e. 25 000) **[1]**
    Computer sales: Solving 2a + 5 = 25, so a = 10 (i.e. 10 000) **[1]**
22. $m = 2$, $c = -3$ **[1]**
    $y = 2x - 3$ **[1]**

    Gradients of parallel lines are equal.

23. **(a)** Sides of triangle $x + 3$ **[1]**
    Perimeter of triangle = perimeter of square
    $3x + 6 = 4x$ **[1]**
    $x = 6$cm **[1]**
    (b) Height of triangle = $\sqrt{9^2 - 3^2}$ **[1 for correct use of Pythagoras on half of triangle]** = $\sqrt{72}$ **[1]**
    Diagonal of square = $\sqrt{6^2 + 6^2}$ = $\sqrt{72}$ **[1]** Therefore equal.
24. $\pi \times 3 \times 2$ **[1]** = 6πcm **[1]**

25. 15% of 260 = 26 + 13 = 39 **[1]**

18% of 210 = 21 + 21 − 4.2 = 37.8 **[1 for any correct method]**

So 15% of 260 is greater **[1 for stating the correct answer]**

> In non-calculator percentage questions, there can be several ways to get the correct answer. Here 18% = 20% − 2% or 10% + 5% + 3%. Make sure your working is clear.

26. 75mph = 75 ÷ 5 × 8 = 120km/h **[1]**

36m/s = 36 ÷ 1000 × 60² **[1]** = 130km/h (sufficient accuracy for comparison)

Peregrine falcon; Marlin; Cheetah **[1]**

27. (a) 240 : 810 = 8 : 27

(b) $\sqrt[3]{8} : \sqrt[3]{27}$ = 2 : 3

(c) Ratio for area is 4 : 9 **[1]**

Surface area of B = 180 × $\frac{9}{4}$ = 405cm² **[1 for correct value]**

28. (a) $x = 4$ **[2]**

(b) (4, 1) **[2]**

(c) (0, 17) **[2]**

Practice Exam Paper 2

1. (a) 42 **(b)** 9 **(c)** 7

2. (a) 19.683 **(b)** 24 **(c)** 21

> Use the power and root buttons on a scientific calculator.

3. A2, B3, C1 **[2]**

[1 for one correct match]

> When the distance is increasing at a steady rate, the speed is constant.

4. 3 × 1.19 = £3.57

2 × 0.17 = £0.34

4 × 0.26 = £1.04 **[1]**

3.57 + 0.34 + 1.04 + 0.45 = £5.40 **[1]**

£10 − £5.40 = £4.60 **[1]**

5. 105 **[1]** and 210 **[1]**

420 = 2 × 2 × 3 × 5 × 7 **[1]**

630 = 2 × 3 × 3 × 5 × 7 **[1]**

> Use prime factor trees to find the two common factors 2 × 3 × 5 × 7 = 210 and 3 × 5 × 7 = 105

6. (a) $6x − 18$ **[2]** **(b)** $x^2 − 9$ **[2]**

7. $\pi \times 3.25^2$ **[1]**

$\pi \times 3.25^2 \times \frac{3}{4}$ **[1]** = 24.887…

24.9m² **[1 for correct rounding and units]**

8. (a)

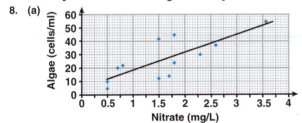

[2 if fully correct; 1 if one error]

(b) Weak positive

> The general trend is the greater the nitrate levels, the greater the algae concentration, but some of the results are still quite far apart.

(c) Correctly read from line of best fit as shown above **[1]**: range 1.6−1.9mg/L **[1]**

(d) Predictions will only be reliable within the range of the nitrate levels in this data (i.e. 0.5−3.6mg/L).

9. (a) $\frac{41.91607978}{7.529536}$ **[1]** = 5.566 887 49… **[1]**

> Work out the numerator and denominator separately and write them down.

(b) 5.57 (or your answer to part (a) correctly rounded)

10. −2 = (−3)² + 2(−3) − 5 **[1]**

−2 = 9 − 6 − 5

−2 = −2 **[1]**

> Substitute $x = −3$ and $y = −2$ into the equation. Remember negative integer rules.

11. $\frac{1}{3} \times \frac{1}{3}$ **[1]** $= \frac{1}{9}$ **[1]**

12. Any suitable answer, e.g.

[2 if fully correct; 1 for two medium triangles shaded plus one or two smaller triangles]

> Each of the larger triangles is worth $\frac{4}{16}$ of the whole shape.

13. (a) 195 **(b)** 195 ⩽ d < 205

14. 7, 12, 17, 22 **[2]**

15. 60 : 100 = 3 : 5 **[1 for correct ratio]**

5.4 × $\frac{5}{3}$ **[1]** = 9m **[1 for answer and units]**

> You may use another correct method, e.g. 60cm × 5.4 = 900cm = 9m

16. (a) First farm (no sale): 0.6 **[1]**

Second farm (from top to bottom): 0.4, 0.6, 0.4, 0.6 **[1]**

(b) 1 − (0.6 × 0.6) **[1]** = 1 − 0.36 = 0.64 **[1]**

> Calculate 1 − P(no sale, no sale)

17. (a) The temperature starts at 100°C and falls **[1]** to about 60°C **[1]**.

(b) Any answer in the range 22°C−25°C

(c) The curve levels out / the custard does not cool as quickly **[1]**. It stays at about 20°C / room temperature **[1]**.

18. $5y − xy = 10x − 2$ **[1]**

$5y + 2 = 10x + xy$ **[1]**

$5y + 2 = x(10 + y)$ **[1]**

$x = \frac{5y + 2}{10 + y}$ **[1]**

19. 2($\pi \times 5.2^2$) **[1]** + 2 × $\pi \times 5.2 \times 7.5$ **[1]** = 414.941… cm²

= 415cm² **[1]**

20. sin R = $\frac{3.7}{5.8}$ **[1]** = 0.6379…

sin⁻¹$\frac{3.7}{5.8}$ = 39.6377… **[1]** = 39.6° **[1 for correct rounding and degree symbol]**

21. (a) 1 : 9

(b) 10800 ÷ 27 **[1]** = 400ml (or 400cm³) **[1]**

22. $m = −2$ **[1]**

$−1 = −2 \times 8 + c$ **[1]**

$c = 15$ **[1]**

$y = −2x + 15$ **[1]**

23. (a) $\frac{27}{9}$ **[1]** = 3

9 + 7 = 16 **[1 for adding parts]**

3 × 16 = 48kg **[1]**

(b) 10⁶cm³ in 1m³ **[1]**

8900 × 1000g **[1]**

8900 × 1000 ÷ 1000 000 **[1]** = 8.9g/cm³ **[1]**

24. ∠BAC = 50° **[1]** (alternate angles are equal)

∠BCA = 180 − (50 + 75) = 55° (angle sum of a triangle = 180°)

∠BCD = 180 − (55 + 80) = 45° (angles on a straight line = 180°)

[1 for correct answer; 1 for three correct reasons]

Practice Exam Paper 3

1. Any eight parts shaded.

2. (a) $-7, -5, -3, 0, 3, 7$
   (b) $0.03, 0.3, 0.309, 0.33, 0.39$

3. (a) 350
   (b) 0.305

   > The second zero is significant as it comes after the first significant figure.

4. (a) $180 = 2 \times 2 \times 45$ **[1]**
   $180 = 2 \times 2 \times 3 \times 3 \times 5$ **[1]**
   Use prime factor trees.

   (b) $2^2 \times 3^2 \times 5$

5.
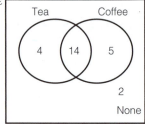

   [3 if fully correct; 2 if three numbers correct;
   1 if two numbers correct]

   > Make sure all the numbers sum to 25. The numbers inside 'Tea' should sum to 18 and the numbers inside 'Coffee' should sum to 19. If the three numbers in the circles don't add up to 25, then there must be some pensioners who don't like either.

6. $(2.95 + 6.50 + 2.25) \times 2$ **[1]**
   £23.40 **[1]**

7. A3, B2, C1 **[2]**
   [1 for one correct match]

8. (a) 89.25kg
   (b) $89.25\text{kg} \leqslant W < 89.35\text{kg}$ **[1]** [1 for correct symbols]

   > The error interval is half a decimal place above and below 89.3

9. $425 \times 0.88 = £374$
   [2 for correct answer; 1 for any correct method]

   > The multiplier method or working out 12% and subtracting are both correct. If you use a mental method on a calculator paper, you must get the answer correct to gain any marks.

10. $6 + 4 = 10$ or $3 : 2$ and $3 + 2 = 5$ **[1]**
    $\dfrac{80}{5}$ or $\dfrac{80}{10}$ **[1]**
    James £48, Jamila £32
    Difference £16 **[1]**

11. (a) Lysette, as she has done more coin flips.

    (b) $\dfrac{44}{120} \times 600$ **[1]** $= 220$ **[1]**

    > Use both of their results added together to get the best estimate.

12. $3x + 4 > 19 \Rightarrow x > 5$ **[1]**
    $2x - 1 < 13 \Rightarrow x < 7$ **[1]**
    So $x = 6$ **[1]**

13. (a)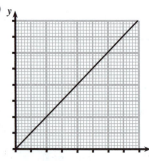

    [1 for straight line with positive gradient; 1 for line from (0, 0)]

    (b)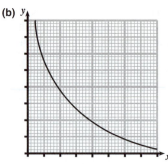

    [1 for concave curve; 1 for lines approaching but not touching axes]

14. (a) 3^{-5} (b) 7.02×10^{-5} (c) $\dfrac{1}{36}$ (or 0.0277...)

    > Remember the index rules.

15. (a) [1 for correct use of scale]
    Answer in range 420−450km **[1]**

    (b) Using your answer from part (a) (for example we are using 440km) $\dfrac{700}{440} = 1.590 = 159\%$ Answer in range 155−165%

    [1 for correct division; 1 for correct percentage]

    (c) $\dfrac{700}{11} = 63.64 = 64\text{kmh}^{-1}$ or 64km/h

    [1 for method; 1 for correct answer; 1 for correct unit]

16. (a) $40 \leqslant h < 60$
    (b) Midpoints (10, 30, 50, 70, 100) **[1]**
    Sum of frequency × Midpoints = 7000 **[1]**
    $7000 \div 140 = 50\text{cm}$ **[1]**
    (c) Correct calculation of $42 \div 140 = 30\%$ or $\dfrac{3}{10}$ **[1]**

    So the data does not support the farmer's claim. **[1]**

17. $(x + 9)(x - 3) = 0$ **[2]**
    $x = -9$ **[1]**
    $x = 3$ **[1]**

18. (a) 44 800km/h

    > There should be four digits after the first 4.

    (b) $(44\,800 \times 3) \div 2$ **[1]** $= 67\,200$ **[1]** $= 6.72 \times 10^4\text{km}$ **[1]**

    > Remember to put your answer back into standard form, with any relevant units.

19. (a) 4.5, 6, 7.5, 9 **[4]**

    (b) Attempt to solve $\dfrac{3x + 9}{2} = x$ **[1]**
    $x = -9$ **[1]**

20. (a) $\tan CAB = \dfrac{2.1}{3.8}$ **[1]** $= 0.5526....$

    $CAB = \tan^{-1}\dfrac{2.1}{3.8} = 28.9°$ **[1]** (3 s.f.)

    (b) $AC^2 = 3.8^2 + 2.1^2$ **[1]** $= 18.85$

    $AC = \sqrt{3.8^2 + 2.1^2} = 4.3416...$ **[1]** cm

    Area $= \dfrac{AC \times 2.5}{2}$ **[1]** $= 5.43\text{cm}^2$

    [1 including units but accept 5.427 or better]

21. (a) £18 000
    (b) $18\,000 \times 0.85 \times 0.85$ **[1]** $= £13\,005$ **[1]**
    (c) $18\,000 \times 0.85^4$ **[1]** $= £9396.11$ **[1]**
    4 years **[1]**

22.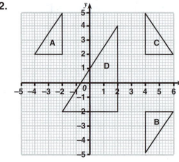

    (a) [2 if fully correct; 1 for correct size and orientation]

    (b) [2 if fully correct; 1 for correct size and orientation]

    (c) [2 if fully correct; 1 for correct size and orientation]